G000081292

PENGUIN PASSNOTES

The Importance of Being Earnest

Iona McGregor was educated at Bristol University and
worked until recently as a teacher in Edinburgh. She has
published several historical novels and educational books
for young people.

PENGUIN PASSNOTES

OSCAR WILDE

The Importance of
Being Earnest

IONA McGREGOR
ADVISORY EDITOR: STEPHEN COOTE, M.A., PH.D.

PENGUIN BOOKS

Penguin Books Ltd, Harmondsworth, Middlesex, England
Viking Penguin Inc., 40 West 23rd Street, New York, New York 10010, U.S.A.
Penguin Books Australia Ltd, Ringwood, Victoria, Australia
Penguin Books Canada Limited, 2801 John Street, Markham, Ontario, Canada L3R 1B4
Penguin Books (N.Z.) Ltd, 182–190 Wairau Road, Auckland 10, New Zealand

First published 1987

Made and printed in Great Britain by
Richard Clay Ltd, Bungay, Suffolk
Filmset in Monophoto Ehrhardt

Contents

To the Student

This book is designed to help you with your O level, C.S.E. or G.C.S.E. English Literature examination. It contains a synopsis of the plot, a glossary of the more unfamiliar words and phrases and a commentary on some of the issues raised by the text. An account of the writer's life is also included for background.

Page references in parentheses are to the Penguin edition of *The Importance of Being Earnest and Other Plays*.

When you use this book, remember that it is no more than an aid to your study. It will help you find passages quickly and perhaps give you some ideas for essays. But remember: *This book is not a substitute for reading the play and it is your response and your knowledge that matter.* These are the things the examiners are looking for, and they are also the things that will give you the most pleasure. Show your knowledge and appreciation to the examiner, and show them clearly.

Introduction

The Importance of Being Earnest was the last of four highly successful social comedies written by Oscar Wilde for the London stage in the early 1890s.

Wilde had already made some unsuccessful attempts to establish himself as a playwright. Two plays had been produced some years before in America, and in 1891 he wrote *Salome* in French for the great actress Sarah Bernhardt. Arrangements had already been made to put it on at the Palace Theatre in London when the Lord Chamberlain forbade its public performance on the grounds of blasphemy.

Oscar Wilde was born in Dublin on 16 October 1854. His father was a physician with an international reputation and also a famous amateur archaeologist. His mother, who wrote under the name of 'Speranza', was a well-known poetess, society hostess and fervent Irish nationalist. Both Wilde's parents were as famed for their personal eccentricities as for more conventional achievements, and Oscar certainly inherited his large frame and flamboyant personality from his mother.

After meeting with great academic success at Trinity College, Dublin, and Magdalen College, Oxford, Wilde settled in London to follow a literary career. He was extremely versatile. Between 1879 and 1891 he turned his hand to producing critical reviews on art and literature, verse and essay writing, and he published fairy tales of which *The Happy Prince* is the best known. He wrote one novel, *The Picture of Dorian Gray* (1891), which was savagely attacked by some critics for alleged decadence and immorality.

However, to his contemporaries Wilde was known less as a writer than as a brilliant conversationalist and master of witty repartee. This reputation was acquired largely at the dinner tables of fashionable London society and aristocratic country houses, where his cynical and outrageous remarks were eagerly awaited and repeated.

Wilde revelled in this attention. He deliberately tried to shock and amuse people by his unconventional dress and behaviour. He himself was to say later that he had put his genius into his life and only his talent into his works. A strong streak of exhibitionism was natural to him, and in addition his attitudes were much influenced by the *aesthetic movement*, with which he became identified. This cult was encouraged by the teaching of the art critic and lecturer, John Ruskin, and an Oxford don called Walter Pater. Pater's writings exalted the study of pure beauty – 'art for art's sake' – and the exploration of personal sensation and experience as the highest good.

Only the most exaggerated and superficial aspects of the movement were grasped by the general public – and, it must be said, by some of its followers as well – and they were gleefully caricatured in the magazine *Punch* by the artist George du Maurier. Du Maurier's affected characters came to look more and more like Oscar Wilde.

When *Patience* appeared, a comic opera by Gilbert and Sullivan, everyone knew that Wilde was its chief target. Wilde himself was delighted with the fun poked at him in *Patience*. He undertook a lecture tour in America as publicity for a production there, but the tour turned into a most successful publicity stunt for Oscar Wilde.

His closest friends knew that under the mask of the posturing dandy there was a warm, tolerant and generous nature. He had no spite or envy in his make-up, and he could not perceive these qualities in others. His arrogant public behaviour alienated a good many people in the circles in which he moved; success made him overestimate the extent to which he was accepted in high English society. When disaster struck, the aristocratic families who had lionized Wilde ruthlessly withdrew their support.

In February 1892, Wilde had his first great dramatic success with the production of *Lady Windermere's Fan* at the St James's Theatre, London. He followed this with two more equally witty comedies, *A Woman of No Importance* (April 1893) and *An Ideal Husband* (January 1895). In February 1895 he reached the climax of his dramatic career. Some critics had grumbled that in Wilde's plays the action was held up by the brilliant speeches and epigrams. With the appearance of *The Importance of Being Earnest* they admitted – except for George Bernard Shaw – that he had written a masterpiece.

It was at this moment that Wilde's life fell into ruins. In 1891 he had met Lord Alfred Douglas, the youngest son of the eccentric and violent Marquess of Queensberry. Lord Alfred was young and strikingly handsome; he was an athlete and talented minor poet. Wilde became infatuated with him almost instantly, and a close, and certainly for some time homosexual, friendship developed between them.

It is probable that Wilde was first drawn into homosexual circles at Oxford. He married in 1884 – happily for a short time – and was devoted to his two sons, but, possibly from the mid-1880s, he became increasingly involved in the 'gay' side of literary life in London and Paris.

The Marquess took a great dislike to the friendship between Wilde and 'Bosie', as his son was known. He harassed them publicly, and tried to disrupt the opening night of *The Importance of Being Earnest*. Shortly afterwards Wilde unwisely let himself be drawn into a libel action against the Marquess, who had left an insulting note for him at his club.

A series of trials followed, during which it came to light that besides his friendships with suspected homosexual men, Wilde had also been spending time with male prostitutes. Understandably, perhaps, but foolishly, he kept this fact from the barrister who was acting for him. The Marquess made full use of this evidence, and as male homosexual activities of any kind were at that time illegal, a warrant was sent out for Wilde's arrest.

It would have been possible for Wilde to avoid being arrested by taking the boat-train to France, but he sat on in a hotel room, apparently stupefied, while his friends vainly urged him to make his escape. It has been suggested that this may have been caused partly by shock, and partly by the wish to play out this real-life drama to its tragic end. Wilde was sentenced to two years' imprisonment with hard labour.

His harsh experience produced a profound change in Wilde. He wrote about it in the moving *Ballad of Reading Gaol* and in *De Profundis*, an open letter to Lord Alfred Douglas analysing their relationship. After being released Wilde spent most of his time in France. He published nothing more, and died of meningitis in Paris on 30 November 1900.

The Importance of Being Earnest played to full houses for the rest of its run, although as soon as the scandal broke Wilde's name was taken off the playbills – a piece of hypocrisy that in earlier days he would no doubt have relished greatly. For some time even his best work suffered the same eclipse as its author. Today, however, *The Importance of Being Earnest* is constantly revived and holds a firm place as one of the wittiest and most delightful plays that has ever appeared on the English stage.

Like his three other social dramas it is sometimes described as a 'comedy of manners', that is, a play in which the behaviour and values of an artificial society are presented (and ridiculed) through farcical situations and witty dialogue.

In these aspects of his dramatic style Wilde was following the tradition set by the Restoration playwrights Wycherley and Congreve, and later to be renewed by Sheridan. But by the time Wilde was writing his comedies other important themes had been introduced into English drama. For example, the desire to prove that 'the good ended happily, and the bad unhappily' had brought in a moralizing note, although the audience could have its cake and eat it by dallying on the way with the openly sensational themes and scenes of melodrama. Wilde's plots and characters are closely connected with this new element in English drama.

The nineteenth century also saw the rise of 'nonsense' literature. Edward Lear's limericks, the comic opera libretti of W. S. Gilbert and the logical absurdities of Lewis Carroll's *Alice* books still delight us today. It is this second element which raises *The Importance of Being Earnest* so far above Wilde's three other social comedies. The sparkling epigrams and the graceful, witty dialogue are of the same high standard in all four, but in this, his last play, all Wilde's talents harmonized and found their perfect expression as he ridiculed and 'sent up' the stage conventions that he had used to create dramatic tension in the previous three. Even if his writing career had not come to such a sudden end it is doubtful if Wilde could have written anything better than *The Importance of Being Earnest.*

Synopsis

ACT ONE

At the beginning of Act One a piano is being played offstage while Lane, Algernon Moncrieff's manservant, is arranging afternoon tea in the morning-room. After a moment the music stops and Algernon enters. We learn that he is expecting a visit from his aunt, Lady Bracknell, for whom some cucumber sandwiches have been specially prepared. Algernon asks about some champagne, which he thinks Lane has drunk, but the servant turns the conversation to the subject of marriage, and then goes out.

Left alone, Algernon expresses disapproval of Lane's attitude. His friend Jack Worthing enters (p. 254). For reasons at present unexplained Jack is called Ernest by Algernon, who asks what his friend is doing in town. He is also inquisitive about Jack's address in the country, but Jack evades his question by commenting on the cucumber sandwiches. He is delighted to hear that Lady Bracknell is expected with her daughter, Gwendolen. Jack loves Gwendolen and has come up to London purposely to propose to her. Algernon finds this very unromantic.

All this time, Algernon has been eating the cucumber sandwiches, but when Jack tries to join in he tells him to take the bread and butter instead. He says that it is most unlikely that Jack will ever marry Gwendolen: he, Algernon, will not give his consent until Jack has cleared up the matter of Cecily (p. 256).

Jack tries to bluff his way out of this, but when Algernon tells Lane to bring in a cigarette case which he left behind on a previous visit, the truth is gradually forced out of him as he has to explain the inscription inside the case: 'From little Cecily with her fondest love to her dear Uncle Jack.' Algernon exclaims in delight that he is now convinced that Jack is a secret Bunburyist. He will not tell him what he means by the term until he hears Jack's story.

We are told that in his will Thomas Cardew, Jack's adoptive father, had made Jack guardian to his granddaughter Cecily, who lives at Jack's country home with her governess, Miss Prism. Jack finds living up to this responsibility very irksome. He has invented a wicked younger brother whom he calls Ernest. Ernest's misadventures allow Jack to come up to London whenever he wants to enjoy himself (p. 259).

Algernon in his turn admits that he has devised an imaginary invalid friend called Bunbury. He uses Bunbury's ill-health as an excuse to escape into the country when life in town becomes boring, and he wants a little adventure.

Jack denies that he is a Bunburyist. When he marries Gwendolen, he will 'kill off' Ernest. Algernon remarks that he would be foolish to cut off this escape route – all married couples need a pretext to get away from each other.

Their discussion is interrupted by the re-entry of Lane, who announces that Lady Bracknell and her daughter, Gwendolen Fairfax, have arrived. Algernon quickly bribes Jack to invite him to dinner that evening by promising to get Lady Bracknell out of the way for ten minutes so that Jack can propose to Gwendolen.

Lady Bracknell enters (p. 261) with a remark about her nephew's behaviour, and shows her disapproval of Jack. Gwendolen and Jack sit down and talk together, while Lady Bracknell asks for the cucumber sandwiches she has been promised. Algernon and Lane play out an elaborate lie to account for their disappearance.

Algernon wants to escape an invitation to his aunt's house that evening, so he now brings up the subject of his friend, Mr Bunbury. Lady Bracknell is highly displeased. She hopes that Mr Bunbury will not have a relapse on Saturday evening: she needs Algernon then to arrange the music at her reception. Skilfully Algernon seizes this chance to remove Lady Bracknell. He invites his aunt to come into the music-room and look over the music he has chosen for her (p. 262).

When Jack nervously launches into his proposal, Gwendolen advises him to take advantage of her mother's brief absence. Jack finds it very difficult to get to the point and Gwendolen takes over.

She tells him it has always been her ideal to love a man with the name of Ernest, and she assures Jack that she loves him 'passionately' (p. 263).

Jack's happiness is spoilt by Gwendolen's insistence about his name. When he tests out her reactions to other names (such as John) she is quite firm. It would be impossible for her to love a man who was not called Ernest. Jack says he must get christened at once. Hurriedly trying to cover his mistake he changes the word to 'married', only to be reminded by Gwendolen that he has not actually proposed to her yet. Jack is on his knees before her doing this when Lady Bracknell re-enters (p. 265).

Sternly, she orders Jack to stand up, and reprimands Gwendolen when her daughter tells her that they are now engaged. Gwendolen, she says, will be informed about any engagement by her parents. Nevertheless, she commands Gwendolen to go away while she puts some questions to Jack. These are to establish whether Jack is an eligible suitor for her daughter.

After a few ridiculous enquiries about Jack's habits and character, Lady Bracknell comes to the real point: has Jack enough money to support Gwendolen in a fitting style? Jack's answers (pp. 266–7) please her very much. After dealing briefly with his politics Lady Bracknell passes on to Jack's family background. She uncovers a devastating secret: Jack does not know the name of his real parents. His adoptive father found him in a hand-bag in the cloak-room at Victoria Station (p. 268). Lady Bracknell is shocked and horrified. After advising Jack to find at least one parent quickly if he persists in wishing to marry Gwendolen, she makes an indignant exit (p. 269).

Algernon begins to play the Wedding March next door, and Jack furiously tells him to stop. When Algernon comes in he informs him that Gwendolen has accepted him, but that Lady Bracknell is 'perfectly unbearable' (p. 269). Algernon says that he loves hearing his relations abused. He is curious to know whether Jack has mentioned Cecily to Gwendolen, and what is going to happen to the imaginary Ernest (p. 270). Jack repeats that he intends to kill off Ernest, and pointedly assures Algernon that he will not be allowed to meet Cecily – in whom Algernon is showing a warm interest. Algernon is trying to cheer his friend up by suggesting possible amusements for that evening, when Gwendolen returns (p. 271).

Gwendolen has come to tell Jack that she will remain true to him – even if she marries someone else! His romantic origin has made her love him even more, and she is still irresistibly attracted by the name Ernest. She asks for his country address. Algernon overhears this and makes a note of it (p. 272). He immediately begins to study a railway timetable.

When Jack goes out with Gwendolen, Algernon tells Lane to set out his Bunburying clothes (p. 273). Algernon is laughing to himself when Jack comes back, and he explains this as being caused by anxiety over his friend Bunbury. Jack warns him that some day Bunbury will get Algernon into serious trouble. On receiving another of Algernon's flippant replies he goes off indignantly. Algernon is left alone on the stage, very pleased with himself.

ACT TWO

In Act Two the scene changes to the garden of Jack's country home in Hertfordshire. Cecily is watering the flowers, trying to postpone the German lesson that her governess, Miss Prism, is impatient to begin. She reminds Cecily of how much her guardian wants her to improve herself; when Cecily criticizes Jack's serious manner, she rebukes her for forgetting his constant anxiety over his younger brother, Ernest. Cecily wishes that Ernest would visit them – she is sure Miss Prism would have a good influence on him. As another diversion she brings out her diary. Miss Prism tells her to put it away, but is easily persuaded to prolong the conversation, going on to the three-volume novel which she wrote in her youth, and then mislaid. After one final attempt by Miss Prism to make Cecily work, the German lesson is abandoned when the Reverend Canon Chasuble D.D. walks up the garden towards them (p. 275).

Cecily cleverly suggests that the Canon and Miss Prism might walk in the park together – it would do Miss Prism's headache so much good. It was Cecily's anxiety over this, she adds, which had prevented her from concentrating on the German lesson! Miss Prism is surprised, but when the Canon seems about to move off – after enquiring whether Jack has returned from town – she discovers that she has a headache after all, and goes off to walk with him.

They have hardly left (p. 276) when the butler Merriman announces that Mr Ernest Worthing has driven over from the station with his luggage. Cecily orders a room to be made ready for him and waits excitedly to see if the wicked Ernest looks like everyone else. Algernon enters (p. 277). At first, Cecily is disappointed. When Algernon says he is not really wicked, she hopes that he is not a hypocrite. Algernon modestly admits to being wicked in a small way, and pretends to be sorry that he has to return to town before Jack arrives on Monday. When he hears that Jack is going to make Ernest emigrate to Australia, he asks Cecily to reform him (p. 278). He then complains of feeling hungry, and asks Cecily to cut him a flower for his buttonhole before she takes him indoors for some food.

Miss Prism and Dr Chasuble return (p. 279). Miss Prism is urging the Canon to get married and hints very openly that he should look for a mature woman – such as herself. They are interrupted by the sudden arrival of Jack (p. 280). He is dressed in deep mourning, and looks very upset. He tells them that Ernest has died of a severe chill in Paris. Miss Prism regards this as a justly deserved punishment; the Canon is more charitable, although he feels that Ernest's desire to be buried in Paris shows that he did not really repent at the end. He will refer to the sad event in his next sermon, which can be adapted for christenings, funerals, and every kind of occasion.

This reminds Jack that he wants to be christened. After expressing some surprise the Canon agrees, and they arrange for the ceremony to be performed that evening.

Cecily returns to the stage alone (p. 282), and is reprimanded for her tactless remarks about Jack's clothes. She tells him that his brother has come to see him. The Canon is delighted, Miss Prism finds Ernest's recovery 'peculiarly distressing', and Jack, of course, is amazed to be told that he really does have a brother Ernest.

Cecily runs indoors and brings out Algernon (p. 282). Jack seethes with helpless anger as he has to listen to Algernon's smug words of repentance and Cecily's plea that he should shake hands with the returned sinner. When they are eventually left alone (p. 283), Jack vents his fury and insists that Algernon must return to town at once. Algernon at first refuses, but finally agrees to catch the four-five train if Jack will change his mourning clothes. Jack goes off in a temper.

Cecily returns (p. 285), and she and Algernon continue their flirtation. Cecily opens her diary so that she can enter the compliments that Algernon is paying her. When he proposes, Cecily tells him that they have already been engaged for three months. She goes through the incidents of their romance, including the breaking off of their engagement, and shows Algernon the letters he had written her. These, of course, she had been forced to write herself (p. 287)! Now they have actually met, she will never break the engagement again. Besides, she tells him, she has always wanted to love a man named Ernest.

Algernon is dismayed to hear this. He asks if the Rector – Dr Chasuble – is experienced in church ceremony, and rushes off to be christened, promising to be back within half an hour.

Cecily begins to write up Algernon's proposal in her diary, and Merriman enters to announce the arrival of Gwendolen (p. 289). Gwendolen immediately and effusively offers her friendship to Cecily. She is upset to discover that Cecily is no passing visitor but lives permanently in the house and is Mr Worthing's ward. Gwendolen is surprised that she has not heard about this from Jack, and is openly annoyed that Cecily is so young and attractive (p. 291).

The misunderstanding is temporarily cleared up when Cecily explains that Ernest's elder brother Jack is her guardian, but Gwendolen can hardly control herself when she learns that Cecily is engaged to Ernest. The two young women almost reach the stage of direct verbal abuse. However, they have to hold their tongues in front of the butler and footman who have come out to lay and serve tea (p. 293).

There is an amusing duel between Gwendolen and Cecily as each tries to score points off the other without being too openly rude. When Gwendolen asks for tea without sugar Cecily sends her a cupful saturated with it and hands over a large slice of cake instead of the bread and butter requested. When the servants make their exit, the girls no longer try to hide their hostility. Cecily cuttingly suggests that Gwendolen should go away. At that point Jack enters (p. 294).

Gwendolen triumphantly claims Jack, only to be told by Cecily that his name is not Ernest, but is able to retaliate when Algernon enters by revealing that the man Cecily is calling Ernest is really Gwendolen's cousin, Algernon Moncrieff. The young women realize that they have both been deceived, and try to comfort each other. When they learn that 'Ernest' does not exist, and thus that neither of them is engaged to anyone, they retreat into the house in disgust (p. 296).

Jack is furious with Algernon. He accuses him of causing the whole situation with his Bunburying. He is glad Algernon will not be able to use that trick again. And Jack won't be able to pretend he has a brother, retorts Algernon. He begins to eat the muffins on the table. Jack finds this 'perfectly heartless', and again asks Algernon to leave. Algernon refuses to go before he has been given dinner. They wrangle on, and the conversation turns into an argument over which of them has the better right to be christened Ernest. Jack becomes even more exasperated, while Algernon coolly continues eating as the curtain falls (p. 299).

ACT THREE

The action is continuous with that of the last act, but the scene has shifted indoors. Gwendolen and Cecily are looking out of a window of the drawing-room, anxiously watching Jack's and Algernon's reaction to their withdrawal. When they see the young men approaching they decide to keep a 'dignified silence' (p. 300), but they are unable to keep this up when their lovers begin to whistle an operatic tune.

Gwendolen speaks first, then Cecily interrupts her to ask why Algernon pretended to be Ernest. Naturally she receives the reply that it was to bring about their meeting. Jack answers in a similar way, and now the only barrier left is the question of the young men's Christian names. They say that they are going to be christened that very day; Gwendolen and Cecily are full of admiration for their 'courage'.

Merriman enters as the lovers are embracing and announces Lady Bracknell (p. 302). She imperiously orders Gwendolen to come over to her. She has bribed her daughter's maid to tell her where Gwendolen had gone to, and has followed her to the Manor House. She tells Jack that all communication with Gwendolen must cease at once.

She then turns to Algernon and asks if this is Mr Bunbury's house. Algernon tells her that Bunbury is dead – a piece of news that pleases Lady Bracknell very much. She then asks Jack for the identity of the 'young person' standing by Algernon, and is told by her nephew that he is engaged to Cecily. Lady Bracknell instantly moves into action. She wants to find out about Cecily's background, and her questions are answered by Jack with sarcastic politeness. Cecily comes well up to Lady Bracknell's standards. As she rises to leave, and, as if it were of little concern to her, she asks about Cecily's fortune. Jack tells her that Cecily has a large amount of money coming to her, and firmly says goodbye (p. 304).

Instantly Lady Bracknell's manner changes. She enthuses over Cecily and is now entirely in favour of the proposed engagement with Algernon. She thinks the marriage should take place soon (p. 305).

Jack steps in and says that as Cecily's guardian he cannot possibly allow the marriage to take place. He will not give his consent because Algernon is untruthful. He has deceitfully entered the house under a false name, pretending to be Jack's younger brother.

Lady Bracknell tries to brush the objections aside, but Jack remains firm. Lady Bracknell points out that Cecily will soon be of age, so Jack's consent is of little importance. Even when she learns that under the terms of the will Cecily will not be of age until she is thirty-five, she will not give in. Algernon, too, is prepared to wait – but Cecily is not.

Jack then points out (p. 307) that the matter is in Lady Bracknell's own hands. Algernon may certainly marry Cecily as soon as Lady Bracknell agrees to allow him, Jack, to marry Gwendolen. Lady Bracknell emphatically refuses to make this bargain, and rises to depart. At this moment Dr Chasuble enters. He says that everything has been prepared for the christenings (p. 308). Jack tells him that as things have turned out there is little point in going ahead with the ceremony. Disappointed, the Canon prepares to return to the church, where, he tells us, Miss Prism is waiting for him in the vestry.

The mention of Miss Prism's name startles Lady Bracknell, and she demands to see the governess. Miss Prism, however, has grown tired of waiting for Dr Chasuble and has followed him to the house. She enters (p. 309), and grows pale as she recognizes Lady Bracknell.

She tries to escape but is paralyzed by the ringing question, 'Prism! Where is that baby?'

We learn that Miss Prism had once been employed by Lord and Lady Bracknell. Twenty-eight years before she disappeared with a baby and a perambulator. The perambulator was later discovered, but it contained only the manuscript of a three-volume novel.

Miss Prism confesses that she absent-mindedly substituted her manuscript for the baby, whom she had deposited in a hand-bag at a railway left-luggage cloak-room.

Jack rushes out (p. 310) to look for the hand-bag in which Mr Cardew had found him at Victoria Station. When he re-enters holding the hand-bag Miss Prism is delighted to have it restored to her. Jack exclaims that the baby has been restored to her too – and calls her Mother. Miss Prism hotly rejects the name and tells Jack he must find out the secret of his birth from Lady Bracknell.

In this way Jack learns at last that he is the son of Mrs Moncrieff, Lady Bracknell's sister, and therefore Algernon's elder brother! Jack cries out that he always said he had a brother, and tells Algernon he will have to be more respectful to him in future. Gwendolen brings them all back to the important question: what is Jack's real name? Lady Bracknell knows he was named after his father, but that is all.

Jack excitedly goes through the military directories in the bookcase and finds out that his father was christened Ernest John. He turns in delight to Gwendolen. Hadn't he always told her his name was Ernest (p. 313)?

The play ends with the three pairs of lovers joyfully embracing. When Lady Bracknell remarks that her newly found nephew is displaying signs of triviality, Jack assures her that for the first time in his life he has realized the vital Importance of Being Earnest.

An Account of the Plot

ACT ONE

The play opens in the morning-room of Algernon Moncrieff's flat in Half-Moon Street. This is in Mayfair, the most fashionable part of London. We see the manservant, Lane, arranging afternoon tea on a table while a piano is played offstage. When the music stops Algernon enters and chats to Lane about his skill as a pianist. He asks if Lane has prepared the cucumber sandwiches for Lady Bracknell, and then sits down and begins to eat them. Next he questions Lane on the amount of champagne consumed on a previous evening, asking why it is that in a bachelor's household the servants invariably drink the champagne. Lane replies coolly that this is because it is usually of better quality than in married households. Algernon is dismayed to find that marriage can have such bad effects; Lane assures him that he is not speaking from personal experience – he has been married only once and is trying to put the experience behind him.

This conversation between master and man (pp. 253–4) immediately takes us into the artificial world of the play and the high-society background of its characters. Lane is as unflappable as his master. He acts as an audience for Algernon's wit, but rises to it only as far as is respectful. He obviously exacts his price: Algernon does not pursue the subject of the stolen champagne.

Left alone, Algernon shows disapproval of Lane's 'lax' views on marriage. 'Really, if the lower orders don't set us a good example, what on earth is the use of them?' (p. 254). This is one of many 'reversals' – that is, a turning inside-out of an accepted thought or saying. At the time the upper classes were thought of as setting a good example to the lower. Wilde is mocking this patronizing assumption.

Lane re-enters to announce the arrival of Mr Ernest Worthing. This is Algernon's friend Jack, but we are not immediately told why he is known by two different names. Jack teases Algernon about his appetite, and it comes out in their conversation that Jack has been in the country since Thursday, and was very bored there. Algernon makes the first of several attempts to find out Jack's country address, but Jack brushes his curiosity aside by making a joke about the cucumber sandwiches, and asking who the expected visitors are.

'Oh! merely Aunt Augusta and Gwendolen,' replies Algernon (p. 255), revealing his relationship with the visitors. Jack is delighted, because he loves Lady Bracknell's daughter, and has come up to town to propose to her. Algernon's reply shows that Lady Bracknell may oppose this. He also makes some typically flippant remarks about marriage taking the romance out of love.

Algernon continues to munch the cucumber sandwiches but when Jack tries to join him he asks him to eat the bread and butter instead. He tells his friend that it is unlikely he will ever be married to Gwendolen, firstly, because girls never marry the men they flirt with, and secondly, he will not give his consent until Jack has cleared up the matter of Cecily (p. 256).

So within a few minutes of the curtain going up Wilde has established one of the main themes of the play – the contrast between love and marriage. The playful refusal of Algernon's consent foreshadows the objections of Lady Bracknell. We are also curious about the mystery of Jack's double name, and are anticipating the arrival of Lady Bracknell and Gwendolen.

Jack tries to deny any knowledge of Cecily, so Algernon orders Lane to bring in a cigarette case which Jack has left behind on a previous visit. The production of some incriminating object is a stock theme in melodrama. A letter or a brooch or fan all feature in Wilde's other plays and are used to prove someone's guilt. Here the possible absurdity of the situation is exploited: Jack is irritated that Algernon did not tell him about finding the case before, and when Algernon opens it Jack says, 'It is a very ungentlemanly thing to read a private cigarette case' (p. 256).

Algernon teases Jack unmercifully. First he pretends that the case is not Jack's at all as an inscription inside says that it is a present from someone named Cecily, and Jack has just said he knows no one of that name. Jack claims that Cecily is his aunt. Then why, asks Algernon, is the case inscribed 'From little Cecily, with her fondest love to her dear Uncle Jack'? The explanation is forced out of Jack one detail at a time as he becomes more and more exasperated with Algernon, who says accusingly, 'Besides, your name isn't Jack at all; it is Ernest.' In proof he brings out a card inscribed 'Mr Ernest Worthing'. Jack is forced to admit that he is Ernest in town, and Jack in the country. That is just as Algernon expected, and he exclaims that as he has always suspected Jack is a 'confirmed and secret Bunburyist' (p. 258). We have to hear Jack's story before the term is explained.

The Cecily of the cigarette case is Cecily Cardew, the granddaughter of old Mr Thomas Cardew who adopted Jack when he was a little boy. In his will, he made Jack her guardian. Cecily now lives at Jack's country house with her governess, Miss Prism.

Once more Algernon tries to prise his country address out of Jack – for, as we now realize, Cecily has been on his mind ever since he became aware of her existence. Foiled again he returns to the question of his friend's two names. Jack explains that in order to escape the responsibility of the high moral tone he has to adopt for Cecily's benefit, he has invented a wicked younger brother whom he calls Ernest. Ernest lives in London, and has continually to be rescued from his 'scrapes'. This gives Jack an excuse to get up to town to enjoy himself whenever he wants to.

Algernon's suspicions are confirmed. 'You are one of the most advanced Bunburyists I know,' he says (p. 259).

We are now told what this means. Algernon pretends that he has a friend called Bunbury, who suffers from bad health and lives in the country. Whenever Bunbury is ill Algernon has to leave town to visit him. Bunbury is invaluable in getting Algernon out of tiresome social engagements, and leaving him free to divert himself in the country. (Algernon's adventures there are not enlarged upon. We may imagine them as consisting in irresponsible flirtations with young women.)

Algernon says that he intends to use Bunbury to get him out of a dinner engagement with his Aunt Augusta, Lady Bracknell. He has already dined with her once that week and wants to have dinner with Jack instead. He is eager to explain the rules of 'Bunburying', but

Jack says that he intends to 'kill off' Ernest when he marries Gwendolen; besides, Cecily is becoming too inquisitive about Ernest. Algernon advises his friend not to do anything so rash: Jack will find married life very tedious if he does not have some excuse to absent himself. Even if he doesn't, Gwendolen will.

Jack reproves Algernon for his cynicism about marriage. Their conversation is interrupted by the ringing of the front door bell, heralding the arrival of Lady Bracknell and Gwendolen. Algernon hurriedly persuades Jack to agree to their dinner arrangement, promising that he will see to it that Jack has ten minutes alone with Gwendolen in order to make his proposal of marriage.

Lady Bracknell and Gwendolen enter (p. 261). Lady Bracknell is a commanding and forthright woman. She makes a stern remark to Algernon, and shows her dislike of Jack by an icy bow. Gwendolen, however, at once addresses her lover and goes to sit beside him. Lady Bracknell makes a scathing remark about the friend whose house she has just left, and looks forward with pleasure to tea. She tries to separate her daughter from Jack but Gwendolen refuses to move.

Now the cucumber sandwiches come into the forefront – again – or, rather, they do not, because Algernon has eaten them all. He makes a pretence of horror at their absence and Lane loyally tells an elaborate lie about not having been able to find any cucumbers 'even for ready money' (p. 261) – a hit at Algernon's extravagant way of life, which is supported by endless financial credit.

While Jack and Gwendolen continue their private conversation, Algernon excuses himself from dining with his aunt that evening with the plea that 'my poor friend Bunbury is very ill again'. Lady Bracknell is annoyed and expresses herself strongly: '. . . it is high time that Mr Bunbury made up his mind whether he was going to live or die' (p. 262). Algernon is to make sure that his friend does not have a relapse on Saturday; Lady Bracknell is relying on her nephew to arrange some music for her reception on that evening.

Craftily Algernon seizes this opportunity to fulfil his promise to Jack. He invites Lady Bracknell to accompany him into the next room to look over the programme he has drawn up for her. She agrees but shows her intention to dominate the choice of music – as indeed she tries to dominate everyone and every situation she comes into contact with. 'French songs I cannot possibly allow,' she remarks severely

(p. 263). Once more she tries to separate Jack and Gwendolen, telling her daughter to follow her. 'Certainly, mamma,' replies Gwendolen, staying where she is.

The proposal scene which follows allows us to have a closer look at Gwendolen, who so far has made only three short speeches. When Jack makes a remark about the weather she asks him not to talk about the subject. People only bring it up when they mean something else, and that makes her nervous.

In fact it is Jack who is nervous. Gwendolen is very self-confident, and knows what is coming. She has already decided to marry Jack (which makes his hesitation all the funnier), but it would be breaking the social rules to mention the topic of marriage herself. She can only encourage Jack to propose. She advises him to get to the point. 'Mamma has a way of coming back suddenly into a room that I have often had to speak to her about' (p. 263). We are confirmed in our belief that Gwendolen is perfectly able to stand up to her formidable mother.

When Jack stammers out his admiration Gwendolen responds by saying that she is well aware of his feelings for her. On her side she knew she was destined to love him as soon as she heard that Algernon had a friend called Ernest. She assures Jack that she loves him 'passionately'.

There follows a comic sequence of question and answer as Jack anxiously tries to probe Gwendolen's reaction to the possibility of his not being named Ernest. What, for instance, if his name were Jack? Gwendolen is absolutely certain that she could not love anyone except a man with the name of Ernest.

Now we realize the significance of the title of the play. How can Jack persuade Gwendolen to love him when his name is not really Ernest? Again, Wilde is parodying a convention of melodrama in which characters may take an inflexible stand on a point of principle. Here, of course, the trivial nature of the principle is in keeping with the absurd atmosphere of the play.

Jack blurts out that he must get christened at once (p. 264) – no, he means they must get married at once. 'Married?' asks Gwendolen in a surprised voice. Jack is disconcerted, until Gwendolen points out that he has not yet proposed to her. Jack goes down on his knees to make the formal proposal of marriage and Gwendolen warns him that she is determined to accept him. Provokingly, she also chides him for taking so long to reach the point. She thinks he must have very little experience in proposing, and Jack protests that he has never loved anyone but Gwendolen.

At this tender moment Lady Bracknell returns from the music-room (p. 265). 'Rise, sir, from this semi-recumbent posture', she exclaims. 'It is most indecorous.' Gwendolen prevents Jack from leaping to his feet and indignantly tells her mother to leave the room, as the proposal has not yet come to a fitting conclusion. She tells Lady Bracknell that she is engaged to Jack. Lady Bracknell ruthlessly contradicts her. When Gwendolen becomes engaged she will be informed of the fact by her parents. Nevertheless, she orders Gwendolen to go down and wait for her in the carriage while she puts a few questions to Jack.

This time Gwendolen obeys. She knows that before she can be officially engaged she has to let her mother go through the routine of finding out if Jack is 'eligible' – that is, whether he has the wealth and social status to make him a suitable husband for her. Gwendolen goes to the door and she and Jack blow kisses at each other behind Lady Bracknell's back before Gwendolen finally goes out (p. 266).

Now follows the most famous scene in the play. It is also one of the most satirical. Wilde makes fun of the money-grasping parents who turned London's social 'Season' into a marriage-market where their children's high birth, wealth and beauty were traded off against each other. The order of Lady Bracknell's questions is important in underlining her priorities. There is no word of love, nor any attempt to find out if the young couple are temperamentally suited to each other.

Lady Bracknell begins by establishing a superior position. Jack's name is not on her list of eligible young men, although she 'works' from the same one as the 'dear Duchess of Bolton'. She asks Jack a series of mostly absurd questions, with equally absurd comments on his answers.

Does he smoke? Yes. Good, a man should have something to keep him busy. A man who is getting married, says Lady Bracknell, should know everything or nothing. Which applies to Jack? Nothing, he says. This is equally satisfactory. Lady Bracknell despises education and gives her reasons at length.

She then comes to the main point of the interview, which is to find out how much money Jack has. She is pleased to hear that he has a large income, drawn mostly from financial investments and not from land. 'That is satisfactory,' comments Lady Bracknell realistically, '. . . land has ceased to be either a profit or a pleasure.'

In putting this speech into Lady Bracknell's mouth Wilde is hitting shrewdly at the hypocrisy of the aristocracy of his day who had long ceased to resist the entry of wealthy business families into their ranks, but who in theory still despised them.

Almost casually Jack lets slip the information that he does, of course, also own a country house with an estate, and a house in Belgrave Square. Lady Bracknell is even more impressed, but maintains control by remarking that the house is on the unfashionable side of the square. 'However, that could easily be altered,' she decides (p. 267).

Jack's political views also pass Lady Bracknell's test. Now there remain only minor matters, the unimportant question of Jack's family. (Another satirical thrust.) Jack has to confess that he has lost both his parents. Lady Bracknell is disturbed by the news. 'To lose one parent, Mr Worthing, may be regarded as a misfortune; to lose both looks like carelessness' (p. 267).

In an apologetic pun Jack informs her that, 'It would be nearer the truth to say that my parents seem to have lost me . . . I was found.'

To Lady Bracknell's mounting surprise and outrage, Jack explains that he had been found by the man who adopted him, Mr Thomas Cardew. Mr Cardew had been given back the wrong bag when he handed over his ticket at the cloak-room of Victoria Station. Inside the hand-bag was Jack. (The word hand-bag here means a grip or portmanteau, much like a modern sports-bag.)

Lady Bracknell's indignation is magnificently expressed. 'To be born, or at any rate bred, in a hand-bag . . . seems to me to display a contempt for the ordinary decencies of family life that reminds one of the worst excesses of the French Revolution' (p. 268). It is obvious that she will not allow Jack to marry her daughter now.

Despairingly, Jack asks what he can do to obtain her consent. She advises him to produce at least one parent before the Season is over. We see that her revulsion at Jack's bizarre origin is not strong enough to make her completely give up the idea of obtaining this wealthy husband for Gwendolen. Jack replies that the only thing he can produce is the hand-bag – surely that should satisfy Lady Bracknell?

She scornfully dismisses the idea. How could she and Lord Bracknell dream of allowing their only daughter 'to marry into a cloak-room and form an alliance with a parcel' (p. 269)?

Lady Bracknell's splendid exit is the climax of the act, but the final few moments help to complicate the intrigue. Jack is left alone, and next door Algernon most inappropriately strikes up the Wedding March on the piano. In a very bad humour, Jack goes to the door and tells him to stop. Algernon enters and asks in surprise if Gwendolen has refused his friend. Gloomily Jack informs him that 'Gwendolen is as right as a trivet.' It is Lady Bracknell who is causing trouble. Jack does not spell out the details. 'Never met such a Gorgon,' he says, and then apologizes for abusing Algernon's aunt. Algernon waves this away. When Jack asks whether Gwendolen will ever become like her mother (a distinct possibility, as we can see from her strong character), Algernon airily replies that all women become like their mothers.

Algernon now wants to know if Jack has told Gwendolen about his double identity, but Jack pushes this sore point aside. He repeats that he is going to get rid of Ernest. Algernon works back to the subject of Cecily. 'Won't she feel his loss a good deal?' (p. 270). Jack is quite sure she will not. (This is ironic, for, as we shall see, Cecily is consumed with curiosity about Ernest.) Algernon comes into the open and says he would like to see Cecily. Jack is going to make sure he never does, since Cecily is 'excessively pretty, and she is only just eighteen' (p. 271). Algernon asks rather maliciously whether Gwendolen has been told about Cecily. Jack, perhaps aware of what Gwendolen's reaction might be, says the two young women are certain to be great friends. 'Half an hour after they have met, they will be calling each other sister.'

'Women only do that when they have called each other a lot of other things first,' comments Algernon cynically (p. 271).

This exchange neatly makes us anticipate another possible complication – and describes exactly what happens in the next two acts.

Next there is more conversation between Jack and Algernon, in which we see Algernon trying to cheer up his friend. But Jack is so depressed by the setback to his hopes of marriage that he has no interest in the usual after-dinner amusements that Algernon suggests. The interlude also allows the atmosphere to relax for a few moments before the surprising re-entry of Gwendolen. Evidently, she has escaped her mother and insisted on returning to the flat (p. 271).

Gwendolen tells Algernon to turn his back so that she can have a private word with Jack. He retires to the fireplace and Gwendolen expresses her fear that she and Jack may never be married. She declares that she will remain true to him. 'Although . . . I may marry someone else, and marry often, nothing that she can possibly do can alter my eternal devotion to you' (p. 272). So Gwendolen turns romantic convention on its head! She assures her lover that his mysterious background has 'stirred the deeper fibres of my nature', and she is still irresistibly fascinated by the name Ernest. She asks Jack for his address in the country so that she may write to him every day. He gives it to her.

At last Algernon has the information he has been trying to tease out of Jack during the whole act. He writes the address on his cuff (stiffly starched, and detachable), and while Jack and Gwendolen are still talking he has already begun to look up the trains to Hertfordshire in a railway timetable.

In this episode Wilde both lets Algernon obtain the information he needs and pokes fun at another convention of melodrama: the overhearing of some secret which has a vital bearing on the plot. In his other plays Wilde uses the device quite seriously. Here, the absurdity of the situation is heightened, because Algernon overhears while actually in the same room as Jack and Gwendolen. This, of course, is another dramatic device, more appropriate to farce, whereby the characters can hear only what the dramatist allows them to hear.

Gwendolen tells Algernon that he may turn round (he has already done so) and Jack offers to see her to the carriage. When they have gone out (p. 272) Lane enters with some bills for Algernon, which Algernon tears up. He asks for a glass of sherry, and also gives Lane instructions to make ready his 'Bunburying' clothes. He will probably be away until Monday. Jack has told Gwendolen that this is the day when he will return to the country. Lane shows no surprise. He is obviously well acquainted with Algernon's habits.

When Jack re-enters (p. 273), Algernon is laughing to himself. He explains this as being a sign of his anxiety about Bunbury. Jack warns Algernon that Bunbury may get him into a serious scrape one day, but Algernon loves scrapes. 'They are the only things that are never serious.' Jack once more reprimands his friend for his frivolous attitude and goes out. Algernon gives a gleeful smirk as he reads the address he has scribbled on his cuff, and the curtain falls.

By the end of the first act we have met all the main characters except Cecily, and she has been mentioned frequently enough to give us some information about her. The various strands of the plot have been skilfully introduced in a series of episodes of rising dramatic tension; after the climax of Lady Bracknell's exit the reappearance of Gwendolen rounds off the relationship between the characters, and leads to a foretaste of the dramatic irony that plays such an important part in the play. Jack does not know that Algernon now has the address that he has been trying so hard to get out of him. We are left impatient to see what use he will make of the information.

Critics of Wilde's three earlier social comedies complained that the action was held up while the characters exchanged brilliant epigrams. In *The Importance of Being Earnest* even the wittiest or most absurd dialogue pushes the action forward by presenting us with necessary information or by bringing in one of the play's themes.

The background of fashionable society is immediately established by Algernon's conversation with his manservant; his second conversation, with Jack, introduces the first of three love stories that have to be rounded off by the end of the play. The encounter between Jack and Lady Bracknell serves a double purpose: there is satirical contrast between Jack's romantic feelings for Gwendolen and her mother's mercenary realism, and the episode, besides being very amusing in itself, places the mystery of Jack's birth at the centre of the action. Similarly, Algernon's teasing of Jack over the cigarette case leads the two young men to divulging that they are both playing an entertaining but risky game of deception.

Certain points have been made which will be of great significance later. Algernon's interest in Cecily prepares us for the second love theme, developed in Act Two. Miss Prism has been mentioned, and will play a major role in unravelling the secret of Jack's birth. Jack's and Algernon's familiar treatment of each other makes the tussle over the cucumber sandwiches seem like a family argument – very fittingly, as we are to learn later that they really are brothers.

Finally, the dialogue is consistently amusing but varied to suit the different characters. Algernon's speeches are frivolous and cynical. He is presented as the typical young man-about-town living for pleasure and luxury, despite being plunged in debt. Jack is a good contrast: he rarely indulges in witticisms, and his more straight-forward dialogue is natural to someone who lives a little more seriously, and is absorbed in plans to marry.

Gwendolen is self-assured and perfectly in control of herself and the situations in which she takes part. She speaks in an artificial and superficial manner, adopting deliberately contradictory attitudes. She loves the sound of her own opinions. Her speeches carry a definite family resemblance to those of her mother.

The most striking speeches in the act come from Lady Bracknell. They are formal, opinionated, magnificently phrased, and full of unintended humour. Lady Bracknell is on stage for less than a third of the first act, but her presence provides its most memorable moments.

ACT TWO

The scene changes to the garden of Jack's Manor House in Hert-fordshire. There could hardly be a greater contrast to the sur-roundings in which we have been for Act One than the relaxed atmosphere of an English country garden at the height of summer. Yet, as we shall soon see, appearances are deceptive. The country is as artificial as the town.

Miss Prism, the governess, is waiting to give Cecily her German lesson. Cecily is watering the flowers – a task that Miss Prism says should be left to the gardener. The tableau of a pretty young girl among the roses is quickly dissolved as Cecily plainly reveals she is trying to avoid the lesson. She does not like German: 'I know perfectly well that I look quite plain after my German lesson' (p. 274).

Miss Prism takes her duties seriously. She reminds Cecily that her guardian is very concerned that Cecily should have a good education, with particular stress on German. 'He always lays stress on your German when he is leaving for town' (p. 274). We can appreciate the irony of this, because we know that Jack's reasons for going up to town are far from educational. Miss Prism praises Jack's high moral tone – which again we know is assumed – and Cecily observes that her 'uncle' often looks bored when the three of them are together.

This remark establishes that Jack feels no attraction towards his pretty ward – an important point later – and that Cecily is an astute and observant young woman, qualities that make her a very suitable partner for Algernon. Miss Prism however, is shocked; she reminds Cecily that Mr Worthing suffers constant anxiety about his younger brother. 'I wish Uncle Jack would allow . . . his brother to come down here sometimes,' says Cecily wistfully. She is sure that Miss Prism would have a good influence on him. We see that Cecily is as anxious to meet 'Ernest' as Algernon is to meet her, and may perhaps begin to suspect what is going to happen.

Miss Prism doubts whether she could have any effect at all on such a depraved character as Ernest; indeed, she is not sure she wants to. People should get what they deserve. She then tries once more to make Cecily attend to her lesson by ordering her to put away the diary she is about to write in.

Cecily pertly replies that she would forget all the wonderful secrets of her life if she did not write them down, and Miss Prism tells her that she should be able to rely on her memory. Cecily thinks that memory 'usually chronicles the things that have never happened. I believe that Memory is responsible for nearly all the three-volume novels that Mudie sends us' (p. 275).

At this Miss Prism admits that she herself once wrote such a novel and when Cecily asks how it ended she is told, 'The good ended happily, and the bad unhappily. That is what Fiction means.' Of course, Cecily is only postponing her German lesson, but both the diary and the novel have an important part to play later on. Still pretending interest, Cecily asks if Miss Prism's novel was ever published, and the governess tells her it was not. 'The manuscript unfortunately was abandoned.'

Cecily thinks – or pretends to think – that this means the story was immoral or too daring for public taste. Miss Prism explains that she means it was mislaid. (A very Wildean pun!) The remark jolts Miss Prism back to reality and she makes one more feeble attempt to interest Cecily in her German grammar.

Cecily, however, has caught sight of Dr Chasuble coming up through the garden, and knowing Miss Prism's fondness for him she successfully manages to put off the German lesson for good.

Dr Chasuble enters (p. 276). He is a pompous clergyman who uses long, elaborate phrases and makes learned references that sometimes mystify his hearers. When he enters, Cecily tells him that Miss Prism has a headache and suggests that he should take her for a walk in the Park (that is, the land attached to the house). She declares that it was concern for her governess's headache that made her unable to concentrate on her German!

'Were I fortunate enough to be Miss Prism's pupil,' says Dr Chasuble, 'I would hang upon her lips.' The expression means 'listen to someone intently', but Miss Prism seems to think that the Canon refers to some kind of physical approach to her. When she glares at him, he adds hurriedly, 'My metaphor was drawn from bees.' Bees hang upon the lips of flowers to take nectar from them, so the suggested comparison (his 'metaphor') is between the action of bees and the idea of the Canon listening closely to Miss Prism to benefit from the wisdom ('nectar') of her teaching.

Dr Chasuble then inquires after Mr Worthing and compares him favourably with his dissipated younger brother. During these remarks Miss Prism has decided that she does indeed have a headache, as Cecily has suggested, and would like a walk with Dr Chasuble. She sets some work for Cecily, and Dr Chasuble and Miss Prism go off together.

The hint of a romance between these two older characters is to be expanded later in the act. Dr Chasuble's only part in the action of the play is to agree to christen Algernon and Jack, but the combination of the Canon with Miss Prism forms an excellent contrast to the two pairs of young lovers. These preliminary episodes with three new characters (Miss Prism, Cecily, Dr Chasuble) are amusing in themselves, key in several important points and also provide an interesting but less intense period of action before the mistakes and deceptions of the act work up to their full comic potential.

Left alone, Cecily shows a startling display of petulance, throwing her books down violently. The butler, Merriman, enters with a visiting card from 'Mr Ernest Worthing'. This is the card that Algernon showed Jack in Act One. Cecily is delighted. She gives orders for a room to be prepared for Ernest to make sure that the visit is prolonged, and she wonders if this wicked young man will look disappointingly like everyone else (p. 277).

Algernon enters and Cecily greets him as 'my wicked cousin Ernest'. When Algernon protests that he is not really wicked, Cecily feels let down, and hopes that he is not a hypocrite simply pretending to be bad when he is good all the time. (This is another Wildean reversal.) Algernon is taken aback but recovers quickly and admits to having been 'very bad in my own small way', although he says it is much pleasanter to be in the garden with Cecily.

Cecily is puzzled that Ernest has arrived so unexpectedly, since 'Uncle Jack' will not be there until Monday afternoon. Algernon naturally means to disappear before Jack arrives, but Cecily says he should wait for him because his brother 'wants to speak to you about your emigrating'. Algernon discovers that Jack has decided to get rid of Ernest by sending him off to Australia. Under this threat, Algernon decides that he will reform himself – with the help of Cecily. 'I feel better already,' he says. 'You are looking a little worse,' replies Cecily, and is told that that is because Algernon is feeling hungry. They prepare to go indoors to find him something to eat, but first of all Algernon asks for a flower for his buttonhole (p. 279). Cecily offers him a yellow rose; Algernon prefers to have a pink one – 'Because you are like a pink rose, Cousin Cecily.' They exchange a few more remarks and then pass into the house as Miss Prism and Dr Chasuble return.

The end of this first episode between Algernon and Cecily strikes a true romantic note, unmixed with satire – possibly the only such passage in the whole play. It forms a delightful contrast to the conversation that follows immediately, between Miss Prism and Dr Chasuble (p. 279). The dialogue between these two has also taken a personal turn. Miss Prism is trying to manoeuvre the unmarried clergyman into proposing to her. She points out that a single man is a 'permanent public temptation'. He leads weaker vessels – women – astray by being available as a married man would not. She urges him to find a mature woman. 'Ripeness can be trusted. Young women are green,' she observes. Dr Chasuble, taking 'green' in its sense of 'sexually inexperienced', appears shocked. 'I spoke horticulturally,' Miss Prism explains hastily. 'My metaphor was drawn from fruits.' So she echoes his own earlier remark about hanging from her lips.

Now Jack enters from the back of the garden (p. 280). He is dressed in deep black as a sign of mourning. We already know that Algernon is running a risk by posing as Ernest, and will probably be found out. Yet we have been told twice that Jack is not expected until Monday. His sudden arrival and unawareness that Algernon has preceded him to the country whips up the comic expectation to new heights. What will happen when the two deceivers run into each other?

Jack tells the Canon and Miss Prism that his brother Ernest has died of a severe chill in Paris. He had received a telegram about it the previous night. Miss Prism, severe as usual, remarks, 'As a man sows, so shall he reap.' The Canon begs her to be charitable. No one is perfect – he himself is susceptible to draughts! He feels misgivings when he hears that Ernest is to be buried in Paris. 'I fear that hardly points to any very serious state of mind at the last.' Nevertheless, he will mention it in his sermon next Sunday – a sermon that can be adapted to any kind of occasion such as christenings, celebrations, and confirmations (p. 281).

This reminds Jack that he wants to be christened Ernest so that he will not have to tell Gwendolen his real name, and he asks Dr Chasuble if he knows how to perform a christening. Miss Prism tells him that it is one of the Rector's most constant duties since despite her advice the poorer classes are always producing babies, which they cannot afford.

The Canon learns with surprise that Jack is making this inquiry on his own behalf, but agrees that 'The sprinkling, and, indeed, the immersion of adults is a perfectly canonical practice.' He will do it provided Jack has not been christened before. Jack is rather put out at the mention of immersion – being totally submerged in water – but Dr Chasuble reassures him that he need only be sprinkled. Indeed, such a course is advisable as the weather changes so much. Perhaps he is afraid that Jack may succumb to the same illness as his brother!

Jack wants to be christened in a hurry, and suggests that he should 'trot round' at about 5 p.m. He is put off when he hears that the Canon is to christen twins at the same time, and suggests coming to the church half an hour later. The Canon agrees, and as he leaves he solemnly begs Jack not to be too distressed over his sad loss. Ernest's death may be a blessing in disguise. 'A blessing of an extremely obvious kind,' remarks Miss Prism (p. 282).

Wilde now brings the Ernest theme to its farcical climax. The first half of Act Two turns on what will happen when Algernon is caught out Bunburying by Jack. Wilde increases the comedy of the situation by making sure that the discovery is made when circumstances prevent Jack from speaking frankly to his impertinent young friend. He cannot risk his own lies being found out by other people. The confrontation is further delayed by making the first glimmer of the truth come to Jack through Cecily.

Cecily now reappears in the garden, presumably having left Algernon still eating his meal inside the house (p. 282). She is surprised at Jack's unexpected return home, and then tells him to go and change his 'horrid clothes'. Dr Chasuble is embarrassed at this tactless remark, and Jack gives his ward a sad kiss. We know that his hypocritical grief is about to receive a nasty shock.

'I have got such a surprise for you,' prattles Cecily. 'Who do you think is in the dining-room? Your brother!'

Jack is so startled that he retorts that he has not got a brother. The joke is prolonged by Cecily's misunderstanding of the remark. However badly Ernest has behaved, she pleads, it would be heartless to disown him. While she rushes indoors to bring Ernest out to Jack, the Canon and Miss Prism comment on the false report of Ernest's death. Jack is speechless at finding that his imaginary brother not only refuses to die but is about to materialize before him.

Algernon and Cecily enter hand in hand. With smug mock-repentance Algernon vows that he intends to lead a better life in the future. Jack refuses to take 'Ernest's' hand and fumes with helpless rage while Cecily begs him to forgive the repentant sinner (p. 283). After all, she says, there is good in everyone, and Ernest is so kind to his sick friend, Mr Bunbury! In the end, under Cecily's threat that she will never forgive him unless he does, Jack shakes Algernon's hand.

Dr Chasuble suggests that they should withdraw and leave the two brothers together, while Cecily comments with great self-satisfaction, 'My little task of reconciliation is over.' The Canon, Miss Prism and Cecily go off, leaving Jack to give way to his wrath.

Algernon is in a strong position. He knows, and Jack knows too, that if Jack exposes him he can expose Jack. Jack's first outburst is interrupted by the entry of Merriman. He has unpacked Mr Ernest's luggage and put it in the room next to Jack's. 'I am afraid I can't stay more than a week this time,' puts in Algernon impudently. Jack tells Merriman that Ernest has been called back to town suddenly, and that he is to be taken to the station at once.

Algernon does not, of course, contradict Jack in front of the butler, but he has no intention of going away. When Jack tries to blackmail him into leaving by appealing to him as a gentleman, Algernon remains cheerfully unmoved. He rubs salt into the wound by observing, 'Well, Cecily is a darling.' When Jack orders him not to refer to Miss Cardew in that way Algernon diverts the conversation into an argument about Jack's mourning clothes. He makes an insincere promise to go back to London on an afternoon train if Jack will change them. Jack is so aware of the weakness of his position that he goes out with the lame words, 'This Bunburying . . . has not been a great success for you' (p. 285).

We, however, know differently. Algernon has established his right to pose as Ernest and there is nothing that Jack can do about it. 'I'm in love with Cecily, and that is everything,' he tells himself. 'But I must see her before I go, and make arrangements for another Bunbury.'

Cecily has been lurking in the background to see how the meeting of the two 'brothers' would turn out. She pretends she has returned to water the roses. When Algernon tells her that Jack is going to send him away, Cecily says that their parting will be painful because she and Algernon have only just met. 'The absence of old friends one can endure with equanimity. But even a momentary separation from anyone to whom one has just been introduced is almost unbearable' (p. 285).

Merriman comes in again to announce that the dog-cart is ready to take Algernon to the station, but Cecily says it can wait for five minutes. This is a touching moment; however, the romantic tone is not allowed to last for very long. When Algernon begins to declare his love Cecily produces her diary so that she can copy down his words as he speaks. Algernon would like to look at the diary, but Cecily indicates that it is too private – Algernon will have to wait for its publication!

Although the circumstances are rather disconcerting Algernon launches into a fervent protestation of his love. Cecily approves of what he has to say apart from taking exception to the word 'hopelessly'. When Merriman enters again Algernon orders him to have the dog-cart brought round at the same time a week later. Cecily does not try to intervene, although she says that Uncle Jack may be annoyed. Algernon impetuously declares that he cares for nobody in the world except Cecily, and asks her to marry him.

The conversation that follows echoes in outline Jack's proposal scene with Gwendolen. Cecily, like Gwendolen, is perfectly in command of her feelings and dominates the situation, although Algernon is certainly more eloquent than Jack. The chief difference and variation is that Cecily now proceeds to share with Algernon a world of make-believe that she has constructed through her diary. There is great irony here: Cecily now assumes she is moving from fantasy into reality, but this is not the case, because Algernon is not the Ernest she thinks he is. Conversely, Algernon falls even more deeply in love with the real Cecily he has now met, as her inner personality is revealed to him through her day-dreams.

Cecily reacts to a proposal of marriage in the same way as Gwendolen did. The question has already been settled. In fact they have already been engaged for three months! Cecily explains that ever since she heard about Uncle Jack's wicked younger brother he has been the chief topic of conversation between herself and Miss Prism. She had already fallen in love with him before they met. They became engaged on 14 February last (Wilde makes a slight error in the dates here), and Cecily had given herself a ring and bracelet on Ernest's behalf (p. 287).

Algernon is lost in delight as Cecily's fantasy becomes more and more elaborate. But when she produces a bundle of 'his' letters tied with blue ribbon he protests. 'But my own sweet Cecily, I have never written you any letters.' Cecily reproaches him gently with the reminder that she was forced to write his letters for him. She will not let him read them in case they make him conceited. (Another reversal, perhaps. One would expect 'Ernest's' letters to be full of praise of Cecily.)

Cecily is particularly touched by the letters Ernest wrote after she had broken off their engagement. She shows Algernon the diary entry for that date, and says, 'It would hardly have been a really serious engagement if it hadn't been broken off at least once.' She adds reassuringly, 'But I forgave you before the week was out' (p. 288).

Algernon, now quite besotted, tells Cecily that she is a perfect angel and begs her never to break off their engagement again. Cecily affirms that now that she has actually met him she does not think that she ever could. Besides, there is the question of his name. She has always wanted to love someone whose name is Ernest.

Algernon is horrified. He tries to persuade her that other names are equally attractive – Algernon, for instance. Cecily is as firm as Gwendolen was. If he had another name she could respect and admire him – but to love him, his name must be Ernest.

In a panic Algernon asks whether Dr Chasuble is 'experienced in the practice of all the rites and ceremonies of the Church'; when he receives an encouraging answer he rushes off with a hurried kiss, promising to be back within half an hour. Cecily begins to enter his proposal into her diary (p. 289).

This scene between Algernon and Cecily mocks romantic love by giving a picture of it showing the lovers basing their images of each other on complete unreality. Cecily's diary entries demonstrate that she is totally absorbed in the exploration of her own feelings, even when she is supposedly sharing them with Algernon, apart from the fact that Algernon himself has assumed a false identity. There could not be a greater contrast than between such indulgence in sentiment and the shrewd, calculating approach of Lady Bracknell. Yet the nonsensical good humour that pervades the whole play takes the sting out of the satire. We laugh at Cecily, but not unkindly. The scene works, partly because it is only in his encounters with Cecily that Algernon lays aside his cool, cynical wit. He is charmed by Cecily, and so are we. Moreover, Cecily is not merely a romantic young girl. She is sharp-witted and observant, and capable of exploiting the real-life situations in which she finds herself.

The first part of Act Two deals with the consequences of Algernon's Bunburying. The second half brings Jack his come-uppance. Jack has twice shrugged off Algernon's question about whether he has told Gwendolen about Cecily, and he is now going to suffer the results of his secrecy.

As Cecily is recording Algernon's proposal in her diary, Merriman announces the arrival of Miss Fairfax to see Mr Worthing (p. 289). Cecily presumes that this is 'one of the many good elderly women who are associated with Uncle Jack in some of his philanthropic work in London'. Jack, however, has walked off towards the Rectory, so Cecily orders tea to be brought out to the garden and prepares to entertain Gwendolen until Jack returns.

When Gwendolen enters (p. 289) Cecily introduces herself and Gwendolen instantly responds by saying that they will be great friends, and requesting that they should be on first-name terms. Cecily replies to this show of friendliness in a similar manner, although she is not as effusive as Gwendolen. Then Gwendolen tells Cecily that she is Lord Bracknell's daughter. Cecily, of course, has never heard of Lord Bracknell, and Gwendolen goes on speaking about her father while she assesses the situation. She asks for permission to look at Cecily through her glasses. Some misgivings have come into her mind. Gwendolen probes delicately to find out why such a pretty young girl is present in her fiancé's country house. She is taken aback to discover that Cecily is not a passing visitor but actually lives there – and without the company of her mother or any female relative.

It has been made clear (p. 274) that Jack is not at all attracted to Cecily, even finding her company dull, so Gwendolen's rising jealousy is very comic. She says frankly that she would prefer it if Cecily were older and not so pretty. She becomes quite blunt. 'Well, to speak with perfect candour, Cecily, I wish that you were fully forty-two and more than usually plain for your age.' Gwendolen goes on to assert that she would never doubt Ernest's loyalty, 'But even men of the noblest possible moral character are extremely susceptible to the influence of the physical charms of others' (p. 291).

Cecily rushes to reassure her that it is not Ernest who is her guardian, but his elder brother. Gwendolen is relieved to hear this, and harmony is restored. Still a little disquieted, however, Gwendolen asks Cecily to repeat her assurance that Ernest is not her guardian. Cecily says that on the contrary, *she* is going to be *his*. She confides to the puzzled Gwendolen, 'Mr Ernest Worthing and I are engaged to be married' (p. 292).

Their misunderstanding reaches the height of absurdity. Algernon and Jack have both pretended to be Ernest Worthing, and Wilde extracts the maximum fun from the scene between Gwendolen and Cecily as each tries to prove her claim to the affections of 'Ernest', and their veneer of politeness gradually gives way under the strain.

Gwendolen informs her 'darling Cecily' that Ernest is engaged to her. The announcement will shortly appear in the *Morning Post*. Cecily maintains that Ernest proposed to her only ten minutes previously. She supports this statement by showing the entry in her diary. Gwendolen produces her own diary and finds an earlier entry. Clearly, she must have the prior claim. No, says Cecily. Since proposing to Gwendolen, Ernest has changed his mind.

Gwendolen says she will rescue Ernest from his foolish promise to Cecily; Cecily states that she will never reproach Ernest for previous entanglements – once they are married. Gwendolen loses her temper when she is called an 'entanglement' and tells Cecily that she is presumptuous. We can hear the ringing tones of her mother behind the withering remark, 'On an occasion of this kind it becomes more than a moral duty to speak one's mind. It becomes a pleasure' (p. 292). At this point we must feel that Cecily has the worst of it. When she retorts that she calls a spade a spade, Gwendolen sneers, 'I am glad to say that I have never seen a spade. It is obvious that our social spheres have been widely different.'

The quarrel is interrupted by the arrival of Merriman and a footman with tea. Gwendolen and Cecily revert to polite conversation in front of the servants, but each subtly tries to put the other down. Gwendolen makes disparaging remarks about the country and Cecily tries to crush Gwendolen by making her look foolish. She also descends to childish tricks to show her feelings towards this hated 'rival'. Gwendolen refuses sugar in her tea with the supercilious remark that 'Sugar is not fashionable any more' and Cecily puts four lumps of it into her cup. When Gwendolen asks for bread and butter – 'Cake is rarely seen in the best houses nowadays' – Cecily hands the butler a large slice of cake to take to her.

As soon as the servants go out Gwendolen gives way to her fury. She is known for her gentle nature – but Cecily may go too far (p. 294). 'To save my poor, innocent, trusting boy . . . there are no lengths to which I would not go,' cries Cecily fervently. Gwendolen retorts that from the first moment she saw Cecily she distrusted her, and that her first impressions of people are always right. This is an echo (and a contradiction) of her opening words to Cecily (p. 290). Cecily pointedly invites Gwendolen to leave, suggesting that she may have 'many other calls of a similar character to make in the neighbourhood' (p. 294).

This scene between Gwendolen and Cecily is as formally patterned as an operatic duet. The comedy springs from the misunderstanding between the young women, but there is also a deeper, satirical level at which Wilde is ridiculing the insincerity of polite behaviour, which gives way under pressure from real feelings. Wilde shows two extremes: the instantaneous, shallow friendship offered by Gwendolen and the open, virulent hostility that replaces it. In between there is the amusement of watching Gwendolen trying to control herself when she thinks that Cecily may be a threat to her relationship with 'Ernest'; then we have increasing enmity between Gwendolen and Cecily as each tries to prove her superior claim to be his fiancée.

This kind of verbal abuse loses its entertainment value if kept up too long, so Wilde skilfully brings in a restraining influence in the shape of the servants. When the servants go out there is another outburst and it would seem that the situation has been exploited to its limits. But then Jack enters (p. 294).

We know that the deception cannot be kept up any longer, and it is here that there begins the unwinding of the misunderstandings and lies around which the plot is constructed.

Gwendolen cries out to Jack, and he naturally responds to her greeting. He is about to kiss her when she asks if he is engaged to Cecily. Jack laughs at the idea. 'To dear little Cecily! Of course not!' Gwendolen triumphantly accepts his kiss.

Cecily says she knew there must be some misunderstanding. From her sugary tone it seems she is not going to let Gwendolen off the hook. Cecily has realized that something is wrong. She is at pains to point out that the gentleman embracing Gwendolen is Mr *John* Worthing. Gwendolen recoils. 'Here is Ernest,' says Cecily, as Algernon enters. The scene repeats itself exactly. Before she lets Algernon kiss her Cecily asks him if he is engaged to Gwendolen. Algernon laughingly denies the idea in the same words that Jack has used to Gwendolen. Now comes Gwendolen's moment of revenge, as she informs Cecily that this Ernest is in reality her cousin, Algernon Moncrieff.

The two young women, realizing that they have both been deceived, put their arms round each other's waists (p. 295) and try to console each other. 'My poor wounded Cecily!' 'My sweet wronged Gwendolen!' (p. 295). And at last, as Algernon had foretold (p. 271), and after all the mutual recrimination, they call each other sister.

The two couples withdraw from each other. The men walk up and down while the two women embrace, and then Gwendolen demands to know where Ernest is, to whom they are both engaged. Greatly embarrassed, Jack has to admit that there is no Ernest. He has never had a brother, and has no intention of having one in the future.

Cecily and Gwendolen conclude that since there is no Ernest, neither of them is engaged to anyone. (Another verbal absurdity.) They decide to go into the house. 'They will hardly venture to come after us there,' says Gwendolen, and the two young women retreat in disgust (p. 296).

The act ends with a confrontation between Algernon and Jack. Jack is furious with his friend for causing 'this ghastly state of things'. Algernon is undismayed and thinks this the most wonderful Bunbury he has had in his life. The only good thing about the situation, says Jack, is that now that Bunbury is 'exploded' Algernon will not be able to run down to the country quite so often. Algernon points out that Jack's brother is also out of action.

They continue to bandy words, Jack being indignant about the way his friend deceived Cecily, and Algernon replying that that is no excuse for the way in which Jack has treated Gwendolen. The dialogue is full of verbal echo and exactly matched repetition, underlining the point that both men are in exactly the same quandary: Jack wants to marry Gwendolen and Algernon wants to marry Cecily, but there is little chance of either marriage taking place.

When told to mind his own business Algernon jokes back that he would never talk about his own business – only stockbrokers do that. This is one of Algernon's puns, but it reminds us that there is another dimension to their problem – Lady Bracknell's view that marriage *is* 'business'. This aspect reappears in the last act.

Next Algernon sits down at the tea table and begins to finish off what Gwendolen and Cecily have left. Jack reproves him for eating muffins so calmly when they are in such horrible trouble (p. 297). Algernon answers that eating is the way in which he consoles himself when he is unhappy.

There follows a ridiculous argument and tussle over the food left on the table. We are reminded of the scene with the cucumber sandwiches in Algernon's London flat. Once more, Jack in exasperation asks Algernon to leave his house. Algernon refuses. He cannot go without his dinner. Besides, he has arranged to be christened Ernest at a quarter to six.

Jack becomes even more indignant. *He* is going to be christened Ernest fifteen minutes earlier than Algernon. There is no evidence that he has ever been christened, while Algernon certainly was. Algernon, ready-witted as usual, argues that this proves he can stand the ordeal while Jack might find it dangerous. He might even succumb to a chill as his brother did in Paris!

As the dispute ends in absurdity Jack remarks – not for the first time – that Algernon is always talking nonsense. The act finishes with another tussle over the remaining muffins, and another useless plea from Jack, begging Algernon to leave.

Notice how the dialogue in this act becomes more artificial and stylized as the complexity and farcicality of the situation increases. The characters echo each other – not merely picking up distant remarks (Dr Chasuble and Miss Prism) but also mimicking and exactly repeating each other's phrases. The whimsicality of this is emphasized by the country atmosphere of the setting. It also underlines the sameness of the position in which various characters find themselves, for example, Gwendolen and Cecily both being mistaken about the identity of 'Ernest', Jack and Algernon each seeming unlikely to win the girl he wants to marry.

The construction of the act is as elaborate as the dialogue. Wilde manages to extract the maximum fun out of the tangle of misunderstandings brought about by Jack's and Algernon's lies, by an almost operatic sequence of episodes. Let us look at the way he varies the groupings of his characters.

The act opens with two new figures, Cecily and Miss Prism, who are joined by Dr Chasuble, also a new character. Then we witness the meeting between Algernon and Cecily. We have been prepared for this by the references to Cecily in Act One and Algernon's consuming curiosity about her. The encounter comes the nearest to pure romance that Wilde allows himself. There is satire, but it is of a gentle kind, and the flirtation of Algernon and Cecily forms a good contrast to the caricature of elderly attraction shown in the conversations between the Canon and the governess that frame it.

In the central part of this act Wilde builds up the complications like a juggler skilfully adding one ball after another to his display: Jack joins Dr Chasuble and Miss Prism (p. 280); the trio becomes a quartet when Cecily enters (p. 282); the quartet increases to a quintet when Algernon joins it (p. 282).

We then have the head-on collision between Jack and Algernon. Algernon's cool impudence definitely has the upper hand. It is obvious that he will try to stay on to pursue his courtship of Cecily, as he does in the next episode when Cecily reveals the secrets of her diary.

After this there is only one possible permutation left – Cecily and Gwendolen. When the duo here turns into a quartet, with the entry of Jack and Algernon (p. 294), the *dénouement* or unravelling of the Ernest theme begins. Wilde eventually rids himself of this complication: both the fictitious Ernest and (in Act Three) Mr Bunbury are well and truly exploded. But a previous obstacle is now playing a major role. If Ernest does not exist, neither young woman considers herself engaged to anyone.

The act ends in comparative quiet with another food-eating scene between Jack and Algernon. The episodes have been well paced, and the action has never flagged. We are still left with the fundamental question: how are the lovers to be united?

Wilde has kept Lady Bracknell out of this stage of the action. The middle act of the play is an exercise in the pairing of characters, and Lady Bracknell would upset that balance. Her opposition is the final obstacle and it would slow down the pace if she too had to participate in all the mistakes and unravelling that go on in Act Two. We look forward to her inevitable reappearance in Act Three.

ACT THREE

Act Three picks up the action directly where Act Two left off, but we have moved indoors to the more formal atmosphere of the drawing-room, where Gwendolen and Cecily have retreated after learning that neither of them is engaged to Ernest.

Although very indignant, the two young women cannot control their curiosity about how their lovers are taking the rebuff. They are watching Jack and Algernon through a window. Gwendolen observes that the young men must feel some sense of shame or else they would have followed them into the house. She is somewhat annoyed at their apparent indifference, and asks Cecily to cough. However, when Jack and Algernon look round she criticizes their insolence. Cecily notices that they are coming towards the house and she and Gwendolen agree to 'preserve a dignified silence' (p. 300). From the young women's remarks we can guess that they are eager to have their resistance overcome, but pride insists that Jack and Algernon find a way out of the difficulty.

Jack and Algernon enter, and, when no notice is taken of them, they begin to 'whistle some dreadful popular air from a British Opera'. Gwendolen comments distastefully on the noise, but still resolves that she and Cecily will not be the first to speak, immediately reversing this decision by telling Jack she has a very important question to put to him. She now addresses him formally as Mr Worthing.

Cecily anticipates her and cuts in to ask Algernon why he had pretended to be Jack's brother. Unsurprisingly she receives the flattering answer that it was to have the opportunity of meeting Cecily. This is, of course, true, although Cecily does not believe him. None the less she decides she will forgive him because of 'the wonderful beauty of his answer'.

Gwendolen follows this lead and asks Jack whether his deceit was practised so that he could have the opportunity of coming to see her in London. She receives a fervent 'Can you doubt it, Miss Fairfax?' (p. 301). Both young women express incredulity but agree that they must accept the explanations. Ironically, Algernon at least is, for once, telling the truth.

Gwendolen consults Cecily as to whether or not they should now forgive their lovers. Cecily says, 'Yes' and then swiftly corrects herself. 'I mean no.' There is still the vexed question of their unacceptable names. Which of them should have the unpleasant task of voicing this, asks Gwendolen? Cecily suggests they should speak at the same time.

This comic device freshens up what has now become rather a well-worn theme. In unison Cecily and Gwendolen chant, 'Your Christian names are still an insuperable barrier. That is all!'

Jack and Algernon reply to this together – they are going to be christened that afternoon! The young women are overawed at this proof of their suitors' courage and generosity. 'Where questions of self-sacrifice are concerned, men are infinitely beyond us,' says Gwendolen, and the two couples fall into each other's arms.

This inflation of a fairly ordinary act to enormous proportions is known as 'mock-heroic', and again shows Wilde's talent for turning every episode in the play to comic use.

The reconciliation suggests that every barrier between the lovers is now removed. But at this moment we are abruptly reminded of practical difficulties. Merriman enters, coughs tactfully, and to everyone's consternation announces the arrival of Lady Bracknell (p. 302). She has left town in pursuit of Gwendolen.

When Lady Bracknell demands to know what is going on, Gwendolen once more states that she is engaged to Jack. Her mother orders her to sit beside her and proceeds to dominate the company in a long speech. This is completely in character and also tells us how Lady Bracknell knew where to look for Gwendolen. 'Apprised, sir, she informs Jack, 'of my daughter's sudden flight by her trusty maid whose confidence I purchased by means of a small coin, I followed her at once by a luggage train' (p. 302). (Note that Lady Bracknell cannot bring herself to use the vulgar word 'bribe', and that the train is a 'luggage train', since in her world that would be its only purpose. Only an emergency has made her stoop to travel by anything so public.) Lord Bracknell knows nothing of what has happened and thinks that his daughter is attending an improving university lecture.

Lady Bracknell is insistent that all communication between Jack and Gwendolen must stop. Quite sure that she will be obeyed, she turns to Algernon and asks if this is the house where Mr Bunbury lives. Algernon airily explains that Bunbury is dead – he was exploded. In the slang of the time this word meant 'condemned' or 'rejected'.

Lady Bracknell takes the more literal sense and asks if Mr Bunbury was the victim of a revolutionary outrage. When Algernon explains that he meant to say that the doctors had found that Bunbury could not live, his aunt is very pleased that the dithering Mr Bunbury had sensibly 'made up his mind at the last to some definite course of action, and acted under proper medical advice' (p. 303). The whole exchange is one of the wittiest of Wilde's sustained puns.

Lady Bracknell now wants to know the name of the 'young person' whose hand Algernon is holding (Cecily). When Cecily is introduced and she is told that Algernon is engaged to her, she proceeds to interfere in her usual way – although she had no legal control over her nephew. Sarcastically, she asks, '. . . is Miss Cardew at all connected with any of the larger railway stations in London?' We are reminded of her interrogation of Jack in Act One. Her further questions both reinforce the impression of her domineering nature and lead to the disclosure that, in society terms, Cecily is a very suitable match for Algernon.

Jack keeps his temper with great difficulty under this cross-examination. He ironically offers to provide Cecily's certificate of baptism and records of her various childhood ailments. Lady Bracknell proves equal in her rejoinder: 'A life crowded with incident, I see . . .' she comments loftily (p. 304). She has now found out what she wants to know about Cecily's background, and is rather more subtle about coming to the main point than she was in Act One. She rises to go and with pretended casualness adds, 'As a matter of form, Mr Worthing, I had better ask you if Miss Cardew has any little fortune?'

With equal nonchalance Jack replies, 'Oh! about a hundred and thirty thousand pounds in the Funds' (Government securities). He courteously says good-bye to his formidable visitor and tries to see her out.

Lady Bracknell is dumbfounded. She must certainly secure this wealthy heiress for her extravagant nephew. She sits down again. There is cutting satire in the way she is shown now gushing over Cecily and addressing her as 'dear' and 'pretty child'. Nevertheless, she still criticizes the simplicity of Cecily's dress and hairstyle. She inspects Cecily closely and finds 'distinct social possibilities' in her profile; but she must 'wear' her chin a little higher if she is to be in fashion.

Algernon rises warmly to his beloved's defence. 'Cecily is the sweetest, dearest, prettiest girl in the whole world. And I don't care twopence about social possibilities!' (p. 305).

After rebuking this foolish attitude towards Society, Lady Bracknell admits frankly that Algernon has only his debts to depend on – but she does not approve of mercenary marriages. She herself had not been wealthy when she married. She thinks she must give her consent to Algernon's engagement.

Both Algernon and Cecily are far too sharp-witted to do anything except let Lady Bracknell play out her part, and they thank her meekly for her agreement. She begins to make plans for their marriage, and Jack – whom Lady Bracknell has completely ignored during her pronouncements – steps in. He informs her that as he is Cecily's guardian she cannot marry without his consent until she comes of age. When Lady Bracknell asks in astonishment what possible objection he can have to the match, Jack says that he will not let his ward marry a man as untruthful as Algernon (p. 306). Jack goes through a list of Algernon's crimes, mixing up the real point (his deceit) with absurd trivialities such as drinking a bottle of Jack's favourite wine and eating his muffins. Again we hear the words, 'I have no brother, . . . never had a brother . . . and I don't intend to have a brother', which ironically anticipate the final *dénouement*.

Lady Bracknell tries to push Jack's opposition aside by announcing that she will overlook Algernon's misconduct. Jack sticks firmly to his decision not to allow Algernon to marry Cecily. Lady Bracknell then tries to persuade Cecily that the three years that must be borne until she reaches the age of twenty-one will soon pass. Jack points out quickly that under the terms of Mr Cardew's will Cecily does not come of age until she is thirty-five. With callous indifference to the lovers' feelings Lady Bracknell finds that thirty-five is a splendid age to be – half the Society women in London have been thirty-five for years. And by the time Cecily reaches it there should be a large accumulation of property.

Algernon protests romantically that he will wait for Cecily, but she more realistically replies that she hates waiting five minutes for anybody: '. . . waiting, even to be married, is quite out of the question' (p. 307). When Algernon asks despairingly what is to be done Cecily makes a formal reply, 'I don't know, Mr Moncrieff.'

Lady Bracknell now asks Jack to reconsider his decision. There is an ironic contrast between her present attitude and the one she adopted towards Jack in Act One. Jack smoothly points out that the solution lies in her own hands: as soon as she will allow him to marry Gwendolen he will permit Cecily to be united with Algernon.

We see that Jack's attitude towards Algernon's engagement was not moral at all – he intended to use it as a lever against Lady Bracknell. But she will not give in to blackmail. She is affronted and says the idea is impossible. She rises with dignity and commands Gwendolen to accompany her to the station (p. 308).

Apparently we are back where we started. Lady Bracknell will not consent to let her only daughter marry someone 'whose origin was a Terminus' (p. 303), and Algernon will not be allowed to marry Cecily until Lady Bracknell changes her mind about Jack. The situation seems to be at a deadlock.

In fact, the resolution is very near and is to come through Miss Prism. Even Dr Chasuble, the least-worked figure in the play as far as the plot is concerned, now takes a hand in events. He enters (p. 308) to announce that everything is ready for the christenings. Lady Bracknell's mind is still full of the marriage plans made by the four young people, and she asks if this idea of christening is not 'somewhat premature' – that is, it is much too early to make arrangements to christen the children to be expected of these marriages.

When she hears the true explanation she forbids her nephew to go through with the ceremony. Lord Bracknell would be annoyed. We notice that Lady Bracknell is quite unscrupulous about using her husband's name as a threat if she considers it useful to do so – although it has already been made plain that he has no real influence within his family.

Jack tells the Canon that there is no point in going through with the arrangements now. Dr Chasuble, a little ruffled, regrets the change in plan, and decides to return to the church. He tells us that he has just been informed that Miss Prism is waiting for him in the vestry.

The mention of this name has an amazing effect on Lady Bracknell. Is Miss Prism 'a female of repellent aspect, remotely connected with education' (p. 308)?

Chasuble indignantly replies that Miss Prism is cultured and respectable, and Lady Bracknell is satisfied that this must be the same person. She insists on seeing her at once.

'She approaches; she is nigh,' responds Dr Chasuble in words that show Miss Prism has made some progress in her pursuit of him. They also parody the high-flown style of melodrama – very appropriately, since the most sensational revelations are about to be made.

Miss Prism instantly recognizes Lady Bracknell and tries to escape (p. 309). Lady Bracknell's commanding tones crush her into an old habit of obedience. 'Come here, Prism! Prism! Where is that baby?'

Wilde gives precise details on the way he wants his characters to react to this startling question. The Canon is horrified; Jack and Algernon shield the purity of their fiancées from the presence of some terrible scandal. In awesome tones, Lady Bracknell thunders out her accusation of the shrivelling governess. Twenty-eight years before, Miss Prism had been employed by Lord and Lady Bracknell. One day she left their house with a baby and a perambulator. They both disappeared. A few weeks later the perambulator was discovered in another part of London, and in it was 'the manuscript of a three-volume novel of more than usually revolting sentimentality'.

Miss Prism has enough spirit left to be indignant at this sneer against her novel, but she soon has to face again the question, 'Prism! Where is that baby?' She humbly admits that she does not know. On that particular morning she had intended to put her manuscript into a large hand-bag. Absent-mindedly, she put the baby into the hand-bag and the novel into the perambulator.

Jack asks excitedly where Miss Prism left the hand-bag, and, brokenly, Miss Prism confesses that it was 'in the cloak-room of one of the larger railway stations in London' (p. 310).

'What railway station?' urges Jack.

'Victoria. The Brighton line.' And Miss Prism sinks into a chair.

As soon as Miss Prism mentions having put the baby into the hand-bag it is obvious to us that the baby must have been Jack. It should be just as obvious to Gwendolen and Lady Bracknell, but in farce the dramatist can make his characters understand or not understand as he pleases. Wilde uses this device to superb comic effect.

Jack rushes upstairs to find the hand-bag while the others wait in a state of tension. We hear the noise of luggage being thrown about in the room above. Gwendolen observes, 'This suspense is terrible. I hope it will last.'

Eventually Jack reappears with a large black leather hand-bag. Once again we must remember it is a grip like those used to carry round sports equipment. He begs Miss Prism to examine the bag carefully – as if it could have been any other! Miss Prism seems totally unaware of the importance of this identification. She rambles happily on as she recalls little details of her earlier life, and concludes, 'I am delighted to have it so unexpectedly restored to me. It has been a great inconvenience being without it all these years' (p. 311).

With great emotion Jack tells her that the baby has been restored to her too, and tries to embrace her, with a cry of '. . . mother!'

'Mr Worthing! I am unmarried!' replies the startled governess.

Jack misunderstands this as well. He thinks that Miss Prism is confessing that she was not married to his father when he was born. This would mean that she was a 'fallen woman', one of the stock figures of Victorian melodrama. Such a situation was then regarded as very shameful, and more blame was attached to the unmarried mother than to the father of the child. Jack's words parody the emotions that might be expressed in melodrama, where moral outrage could be shown in conflict with pity and a wish to accept the child.

'. . . who has the right to cast a stone against one who has suffered? . . . Mother, I forgive you,' he cries.

Miss Prism is furious at this slur on her virtue and tells Jack that he must ask Lady Bracknell for the secret of his birth. 'Lady Bracknell, I hate to seem inquisitive,' he says to her, 'but would you kindly inform me who I am?'

Lady Bracknell has been unusually quiet during Jack's conversation with Miss Prism. She now moves forward to dominate the final moments of the play. She announces that the answer to his question will not please him. He is the son of her sister, Mrs Moncrieff, and thus Algernon's elder brother.

Jack cries out in elation that he knew he had a brother – he had always said so! Absurdly, he introduces Algernon to everyone on stage as his younger brother – as if it were Algernon, and not himself who had acquired a new identity. He tells Algernon he will have to treat him with more respect in future. 'You have never behaved to me like a brother in all your life.' Algernon admits that he had not done so until that day. But after all, he was out of practice (p. 312).

Gwendolen brings them all back to the crucial point: what is Jack's real name? Jack asks her whether she still refuses to marry him unless his name is Ernest, and Gwendolen answers that she never changes, except in her affections.

When Jack anxiously questions his newly found aunt he learns that he had already been christened when Miss Prism lost him. Being the eldest son he was naturally named after his father. Lady Bracknell cannot remember her brother-in-law's name.

Jack appeals to Algernon, 'My dear boy,' his younger brother tells him, 'we were never even on speaking terms. He died before I was a year old.'

Jack has an idea. Lady Bracknell has already mentioned that his father was a General. As a military man he would have had his name inserted in the army directories of the period. By a fortunate coincidence these are in the bookcase. At last he comes across the entry for Moncrieff and at the end of it finds his father's Christian names – Ernest John. Jack turns to his fiancée. 'I always told you, Gwendolen, my name was Ernest, didn't I?' (p. 313).

Lady Bracknell now remembers that her dislike of the name related to her dislike of the General. Gwendolen is delighted. Jack remarks that it is terrible to find out that he was telling the truth when he thought he was lying. He is both Ernest and John. Can Gwendolen forgive him? Of course Gwendolen can – 'For I feel that you are sure to change.'

Joyfully, the three pairs of lovers turn to each other, crying, 'At last!' It is notable that Cecily is the only one of the six who says nothing – but Wilde has done this deliberately. Cecily must give up her claim. Algernon, obviously, cannot bear the name of Ernest as well as Jack.

The couples embrace in front of Lady Bracknell. She almost has the last word. Quite good-humouredly, she says, to Jack, 'My nephew, you seem to be displaying signs of triviality.' On the contrary, Jack assures her, he has now realized for the first time in his life the vital Importance of Being Earnest.

This last act brings the *dénouement* – that is, all the mistakes and entanglements are resolved, and the characters arrive safely at the happy ending with the three couples united in traditional romantic fashion. Lady Bracknell, who personifies social obstacles, has been persuaded to smile on them and all seem set to 'live happily ever after'.

However, if we look more closely at what has actually happened we will realize that it is Society and its values which have triumphed, not romance. Gwendolen is to marry her cousin, with the result that family property will be kept within a tight little social circle; the penniless Algernon has captured a rich heiress; and the obstinately celibate Dr Chasuble has been persuaded to become a respectably married man. Lady Bracknell can well afford to unbend at the end of the play.

The grouping of the characters is much simpler than in the two previous acts. The action opens with Gwendolen and Cecily, and Wilde brings in the other characters one after another until everyone (except the servants) is on the stage. There are no major exits or entrances except for Jack's brief absence to find the hand-bag.

The action is continuous with that of Act Two, and so is the theme, which is the exploration of the quarrel between the lovers. This is resolved by Algernon's quick tongue, and with the announcement of the intended christenings all difficulties seem about to vanish.

We are brought back to reality by the expected but very sudden entry of Lady Bracknell. The episode where she investigates Cecily's qualifications for marrying Algernon echoes her interview with Jack in Act One. But there is a piquant variation, which underlines the satire in both episodes. After being very cold to Cecily, Lady Bracknell welcomes her with open arms. This leads on to the neat reversal of roles in which Jack opposes the suggested marriage while Lady Bracknell presses for it. Lady Bracknell's attempted exit is an acknowledgement that the situation has reached deadlock. At that moment she is powerless to enforce her wishes.

Next we have the re-entry of Dr Chasuble (p. 308) and then of Miss Prism (p. 309). The confrontation between Lady Bracknell and her former employee is the only one that Wilde has not prepared us for. This will bring the surprise solution to the impasse into which the characters have fallen.

Even now Wilde cleverly delays the end. There is a false climax when Jack thinks that Miss Prism is his mother and much ludicrous parodying of the conventions of melodrama, which Wilde is mocking. Finally, we return to the question on which the punning title of the play has been based. What's in a name? After Jack's secret is out and the lovers are free to express their affection, Lady Bracknell censures – with at least half a smile – Jack's air of carefree happiness. He is displaying 'triviality'. His reply – 'the vital Importance of Being Earnest' – contains a paradox that mocks the contrasts between truth and deceit, appearance and reality, sincerity and cynicism, round which the play has revolved.

The Characters

The characters in *The Importance of Being Earnest* are not fully developed, three-dimensional figures. Rather, they represent the upper-class attitudes and values that Wilde is satirizing. However, with the possible exceptions of Lady Bracknell and Dr Chasuble they are not caricatures but recognizable projections of a society that actually existed. Their speech and behaviour are consistent throughout the play.

ALGERNON

Wilde bestowed his own epigrammatic wit on nearly all his dramatic characters, but in each play there is one person who more than anyone else displays the traits that Wilde himself liked to show to the world. In *The Importance of Being Earnest* it is Algernon – Algy to his friends.

Algernon is the typical charming and idle man-about-town. As Lady Bracknell says (p. 306) 'He has nothing, but he looks everything.' He lives for pleasure, and his imaginary invalid friend, Bunbury, gives him the excuse to disappear into the country in search of even more diversions when he becomes bored with London. When Jack warns him that this habit may some day get him into a serious scrape, Algernon says happily, 'I love scrapes. They are the only things that are never serious' (p. 273).

The nonsense that Algernon talks springs largely out of his bubbling good humour. He is also extremely cool. He refuses to be ruffled by any setback. Even when things are at their blackest, at the end of Act Two, and Jack accuses him of being 'perfectly heartless', Algernon still meets the situation with a joke.

Algernon is very particular about his appearance. His hair is carefully waved (p. 288) and he is fussy about his clothes. When told that Jack has gone to buy him an outfit in which to emigrate to Australia, he is indignant. 'I certainly wouldn't let Jack buy my outfit. He has no taste in neckties at all' (p. 278). His preparations for Bunburying are elaborate (p. 273) and need 'three portmanteaus, a dressing-case, two hat-boxes' (p. 284) to contain them. On first catching sight of his friend at the Manor House he asks him to go and change out of his mourning clothes (p. 284) and also tells Jack that he 'never saw anybody take so long to dress, and with such little result' (p. 284).

Algernon is ready to adapt himself to circumstances rather than meet them in violent collision. The only time we see him even attempt to stand up to his formidable aunt is when he tells her that he does not care twopence about the social possibilities of Cecily's profile. Normally, Algernon relies on deception and his quick wits to see him through any difficulties. He adroitly turns the conversation to the choice of music for a reception when Lady Bracknell is displeased about the way in which Algernon wriggles out of attending her dinner party. In Act Three, while Jack and Lady Bracknell dispute over Algernon's engagement to Cecily, Algernon himself stands by in alert silence, no doubt waiting to make the most of any opportunity that presents itself. He finally gives in to Jack's repeated requests that he should leave the Manor House, but intends to arrange a future meeting with Cecily before he leaves (p. 285).

Algernon, in fact, is quite unscrupulous. He admits, 'My duty as a gentleman has never interfered with my pleasures in the smallest degree' (p. 284). He has no pang of conscience about going behind Jack's back to meet Cecily, and is quite unashamed when his trick of posing as Ernest is found out. He keeps Jack's cigarette case until he can use it to worm out the full details of Jack's secret. He is what we would call an opportunist.

It is Algernon's quick tongue that gets the two young men out of their awkward quarrel with their fiancées. When Cecily asks him why he has deceitfully pretended to be Jack's younger brother, he glibly replies. 'In order that I might have an opportunity of meeting you' (p. 300).

Until he meets Cecily, Algernon's views on love and marriage have been extremely cynical. Supported by Lane, he sees marriage as 'demoralizing' because it affects the quality of the champagne served in a household. He says, 'The very essence of romance is uncertainty. If ever I get married, I'll certainly try to forget the fact' (p. 255). Algernon sarcastically derides 'the happy English home' (p. 260) and believes that 'The only way to behave to a woman is to make love to her, if she is pretty, and to someone else, if she is plain' (p. 270).

However, on encountering Cecily, Algernon is immediately attracted by her wit, beauty and fantasizing imagination. In his scenes with her, Algernon's cynicism disappears and his wit dwindles almost to vanishing point. We may take it that now Bunbury has been exploded Algernon is an (almost) reformed character.

Algernon is obsessed with food. His greediness is a theme that provides some of the most amusing moments in the play – for example, the cucumber sandwiches (p. 255), the wily way in which he manoeuvres Jack into inviting him out to dinner by promising him the chance to propose to Gwendolen (p. 260), his complaints of feeling hungry even when talking to Cecily (p. 278), and the fight with Jack over the muffins (pp. 297–9). His preparations to go Bunburying even include a large luncheon basket! (p. 284).

JACK

Jack is an older version of Algernon, as far as his social position and habits go, but he has little of Algernon's debonair coolness and cynical wit. He can say quite clever things – 'When one is in town one amuses oneself. When one is in the country one amuses other people. It is excessively boring' (p. 254) – but on the whole he is in a serious mood during most of the play. He has a free and easy relationship with Algernon, although he often becomes irritated with his flippancy: 'You never talk anything but nonsense,' he tells him impatiently, on several occasions (e.g. p. 273 and p. 298). He is good-humoured under Algernon's frank and frequent criticism.

Jack's serious attitude springs partly from his natural character and partly from the fact that he is in love with Gwendolen and absorbed by the problems of getting himself accepted as her suitor. He also takes his duties as Cecily's guardian very seriously, feeling that he has to 'adopt a very high moral tone on all subjects' (p. 258). However, he finds the role oppressive, and that is the reason he has invented an imaginary younger brother whose 'scrapes' give him the excuse to come up to London to enjoy himself. He has also (p. 289) managed to convey the idea that some of his time there is spent in charitable work.

Jack is neither as astute nor as sharp-witted as Algernon. He tells his friend (p. 270) that Cecily 'is not a silly romantic girl, I am glad to say. She has got a capital appetite, goes for long walks, and pays no attention at all to her lessons' – a description in which only the last item seems to fit the personality that Cecily reveals to Algernon.

In front of Dr Chasuble and the gullible Miss Prism Jack manages to keep up a convincing show of grief over the 'death' of Ernest (p. 280), but when Algernon enters pretending to be this fictitious brother he can only glare and fume helplessly. He does not do much better when they are alone. Caught out by his own deceit, Jack cannot think of any way to force Algernon to leave his house.

When Gwendolen and Cecily retreat in disgust, on discovering that Ernest does not exist, Jack is thrown into despair (pp. 296–7). It is only by following the lead of his quicker-witted friend that he is eventually able to mend his quarrel with Gwendolen (p. 301). Indeed, Jack's proposal scene with Gwendolen shows that he flounders whenever he is in the grip of strong emotion. It is Gwendolen who has to guide their conversation (pp. 263–5).

On the other hand, Jack shows much more courage than Algernon in standing up to Lady Bracknell. He submits to her first cross-examination politely, knowing that he has to abide by the social rules if he wants to be accepted as Gwendolen's fiancé. He allows himself only an ironic question – 'Do you mean the fashion, or the side?' (p. 267) – when the meddling Lady Bracknell comments that his house in Belgrave Square is on the unfashionable side but 'that could easily be altered'. After the interview he says quite bluntly that Lady Bracknell is a 'Gorgon', and then apologizes to Algernon for criticizing his aunt.

When Lady Bracknell invades his home in Act Three Jack remains polite, but when she refers to Cecily as a 'young person' – a Victorian phrase for a girl of low social standing – he pointedly corrects her. 'That lady is Miss Cecily Cardew, my ward' (p. 303). He outfaces Lady Bracknell's questions about Cecily and begins to ease her out of the house (p. 304). When she reverses her attitude after discovering that Cecily is a wealthy heiress Jack allows Lady Bracknell to launch into her plans for the marriage before he steps in and tells her that Cecily and Algernon cannot marry unless he himself is allowed to marry Gwendolen (p. 307). Finally, after the farcical fun over Miss Prism's hand-bag, Jack slips easily into calling this overbearing new relation 'Aunt Augusta', and rallies to her semi-severity with the last witticism of the play.

Jack is deeply and sincerely in love with Gwendolen. Whether he fully understands her nature, however, is another matter. She is 'as right as a trivet' (p. 269) in his eyes, and 'a sensible, intellectual girl' (p. 273). He does not perceive the inconsistency of his own reactions when Algernon, with irritating persistency, keeps returning to the question of whether he has told Gwendolen the truth about his background: '. . . the truth isn't quite the sort of thing one tells to a nice, sweet, refined girl' (p. 270). A few moments later he is assuring Algernon and himself, 'Cecily and Gwendolen are perfectly certain to be extremely great friends' (p. 271). Algernon is far more perceptive about the likely effect of their first meeting. A faint glimmering of reality comes to Jack after his first interrogation by Lady Bracknell. 'You don't think there is any chance of Gwendolen becoming like her mother in about a hundred and fifty years, do you, Algy?' (p. 269). Algernon clothes his wisdom in an epigram: 'All women become like their mothers. That is their tragedy. No man does. That's his' (p. 270). The perception is lost on Jack, who merely sees it as another piece of 'cleverness'.

LADY BRACKNELL

Lady Bracknell is the dominating character of the play although she is entirely absent from Act Two. She comes over as a positive and ruthless person with no regard for other people's feelings or wishes.

Her standards are inflexible; it is only at the end of the play, when others have risen to her high expectations, that she unbends a little and becomes almost human.

Lady Bracknell is the only main character who does not have any active role to play in advancing the plot, despite the fact that it is her rock-like resistance to Gwendolen's 'unsuitable' engagement round which the action revolves.

The humour of Lady Bracknell's character lies in this complete disregard of any other point of view except her own. Only her own convenience counts; she will try to manipulate every situation to her own ends.

Lady Bracknell is a splendidly exaggerated caricature of the society hostess. In *A Woman of No Importance* Wilde makes one of his characters say, 'Society is a necessary thing. No man has any real success in this world unless he has got women to back him, and women rule society' (p. 116). A little later occurs, 'The history of women is . . . The tyranny of the weak over the strong' (p. 116). And Lady Bracknell advises her nephew, 'Never speak disrespectfully of Society, Algernon. Only people who can't get into it do that' (p. 305). These three quotations sum up Lady Bracknell's view of her own position, although she would certainly not regard herself as weak. She accepts the conventions of her world without question, but uses them to maintain and increase her power. In every situation in which she finds herself, she moves swiftly to gain the upper hand.

She dismisses her husband contemptuously. He cannot live up to his duty to be healthy (p. 262 and p. 265); he does not know about her plans to follow Gwendolen down to the country (p. 302). Otherwise, she mentions him only to back up her own authority (p. 269 and p. 309).

Matchmaking is the chief means by which Lady Bracknell and her kind advance the status of their families. It exists as a device to consolidate wealth and social position. Gwendolen cannot be allowed to decide so important a matter as her own engagement – she will be informed about it by one of her parents. Lady Bracknell assumes that it does not matter how long Algernon and Cecily have to wait to get married provided that Cecily's fortune is secured for some branch of her family (p. 307). She is genuinely astonished when Jack intervenes to forbid the engagement (p. 306) and stubbornly continues to grasp at the prize. The feelings of the young lovers are of no concern to her, because love never enters into her considerations. She does not even brush it aside – she ignores it.

Lady Bracknell is a realist, and has moved with the times in so far as the balance of birth and money is concerned. Cecily's wealth more than makes up for the doubtful background of her guardian: '... Land has ceased to be either a profit or a pleasure. It gives one position and prevents one from keeping it up' (pp. 266–7).

'Dear Lady Harbury' (p. 261) and 'the dear Duchess of Bolton' (p. 266) are Lady Bracknell's acknowledged social equals, but we may be sure that others would be scrutinized very carefully before being given this privilege. Anything unconnected with herself or her own plans receives nothing but contempt. Lady Bracknell regards music as a social device to encourage conversation (p. 262) and she despises education. 'I do not approve of anything that tampers with natural ignorance' (p. 266). Her disdain for Miss Prism is based on this as well as on the governess's low social status. In fact, Lady Bracknell is a thorough *philistine*.

The two interviews which Lady Bracknell conducts with Jack show her as a clear-headed businesswoman who can quickly pick out essential details. Wilde satirizes her mercenary attitude when he shows her change of manner towards Jack and Cecily in Act Two. We have already seen this happen in Act One with Jack, whom she greeted first only with an icy bow. After warming to him with the discovery that he has a good income and is a man of property, she reverts to strong disapproval after she has learned of his 'shameful' origin. Even so, she would gladly overlook this for the sake of securing his wealth for her family if only he could 'produce at any rate one parent, of either sex, before the season is quite over' (p. 268).

The reversals in Act Three are even more striking. Cecily, who is slightingly referred to as 'that young person' (p. 303) when first noticed, becomes 'Pretty child' (p. 304) and 'our dear Cecily' (p. 307) when Lady Bracknell becomes aware of her large inheritance. When she realizes that Jack can prevent this desirable alliance with her nephew Algernon, Jack turns into 'My dear Mr Worthing' (p. 307).

Lady Bracknell displays no emotion when she discovers that she has acquired another nephew, but the last lines of the play hint at a little grudging geniality towards this addition to her family.

Wilde satirizes the snobbery lying behind Lady Bracknell's precise social distinctions. (It must be remembered, however, that although the details are exaggerated for comic effect her views would be shared by most upper-class people of her time.) She keeps a list of young men eligible to marry Gwendolen, and we may be sure that their suitability is based on income. Jack has a house in fashionable Belgrave Square (p. 267) – plus! But it is on the less fashionable side – minus! Jack's political party, the Liberal Unionists, is invited to evening receptions, but is not socially acceptable enough to attend the more prestigious dinners that precede the receptions. Algernon's absence from her dinner party is annoying because it will make the numbers of male and female guests uneven (p. 262). She remarks approvingly about Cecily's family property: 'Three addresses always inspire confidence, even in tradesmen' (p. 304). When she learns that Cecily's solicitors are Markby, Markby and Markby she comments, 'Indeed I am told that one of the Mr Markby's is occasionally to be seen at dinner parties' (p. 304).

The only chink in Lady Bracknell's armour lies in her relationship with her daughter Gwendolen. Within the confines of her social position, Gwendolen runs circles round her mother. When she tries to separate her from Jack (p. 261 and p. 263) Gwendolen ignores her requests. She blows kisses behind her mother's back to Jack (p. 265) and when Lady Bracknell sweeps out (p. 269) with Gwendolen in tow Gwendolen reappears within a few moments. Despite all Lady Bracknell's thunder Gwendolen persists in regarding herself as engaged to Jack.

The most striking characteristic of Lady Bracknell is the lofty way in which she speaks. In Act One, notice how cleverly Wilde elaborates the phrasing of her speeches as she moves from social chit-chat to gradually increasing indignation: high points are her irritation at Mr Bunbury's 'shilly-shallying' with life and death (p. 262); the moment she finds Jack on his knees before Gwendolen (p. 265); outrage at Jack's background (pp. 267–8); and then her magnificent exit speech. 'You can hardly imagine that I and Lord Bracknell would dream of allowing our only daughter – a girl brought up with the utmost care –

to marry into a cloak-room, and form an alliance with a parcel. Good morning, Mr Worthing!' (p. 269).

In Act Three Lady Bracknell is more closely integrated into the comic development, and this makes up for the less strong emotional impact of her speeches. As she cannot force Jack to give his consent to the marriage of Algernon and Cecily, she is a less commanding figure. But she still has some very good speeches, and Wilde puts her back into the centre of the action when we finally learn the secret of Jack's birth.

Lady Bracknell is indeed a 'monster' (p. 269). We laugh at her absurd comments, but she is too impressive for us to laugh at her.

GWENDOLEN

Gwendolen first appears with her mother in Act One. She asserts her independence by immediately beginning a conversation with Jack, of whom Lady Bracknell disapproves (p. 261), and she keeps up this clear-headed, determined behaviour throughout the play. Among the four young lovers Gwendolen is the only one who does not use fantasy to escape the restrictions imposed by Society. She is practical and down to earth, despite her sophistication.

When Algernon says 'All women become like their mothers' (p. 270), he is probably making a fairly accurate prophecy of how Gwendolen will develop. There are clear hints that Gwendolen is a younger version of Lady Bracknell, and she is the only character in the play who can defeat her without effort. She blandly ignores her mother's orders to come away from Jack (p. 261 and p. 263) and is quite unabashed when Lady Bracknell turns up at the Manor House, having pursued her from London (p. 302).

Gwendolen is proud of her fashionable appearance (p. 261) and shows great social poise. It is clear that she loves Jack and means to marry him, but she is also a 'tease' and both these aspects come out in her proposal scene with Jack. Jack is nervous, and it is Gwendolen who steers the conversation in the right direction. Although she advises her lover to take advantage of Lady Bracknell's absence she deliberately wastes time by expanding on her wish to love a man named Ernest. This preference either indicates what one might call the serious triviality of Gwendolen's nature, or is a pose deliberately adopted for amusement, amid the restrictions and boredom of her idle life (p. 263). Then when things seem settled between them, she expresses surprise at the mention of marriage – because Jack has not yet gone through the formalities of a proposal.

This waywardness is shown frequently at other points in the play, such as when Gwendolen returns to promise eternal devotion to Jack even though she may be forced to 'marry someone else, and marry often' (p. 272). Many of her remarks feature this characteristic, for example 'I never change, except in my affections' (p. 312).

Nevertheless it is Gwendolen's determination to marry Jack that holds the strands of the plot together. By insisting that she must keep in touch with Jack she lets Algernon secure the address of the house where he will find Cecily. Gwendolen's appearance at the Manor House brings all the deceptions and misunderstandings to a climax.

Although Gwendolen shares some of her mother's attitudes – notably her disrespect for Lord Bracknell: 'Outside the family circle, papa, I am glad to say, is entirely unknown' (p. 290) – there are marked differences in their views on education. Gwendolen likes to show off her learning. She refers somewhat grandly to living 'in an age of ideals' (p. 263), to the examples of 'Modern, no less than Ancient History' (p. 291), and to 'German scepticism' (p. 301). As a plausible reason for Gwendolen's prolonged absence Lady Bracknell has told her father that she is attending a lecture run by the University Extension Scheme. Gwendolen has a touch of the 'New Woman' about her – a figure that was satirized by the magazine *Punch* in this age of expanding higher education for women.

In Act Two Gwendolen's response to Cecily gives Wilde the chance to ridicule the behaviour of high society. Her inconsistencies must be seen in this light. At first supposing that Cecily is only a visitor like herself, she is disconcerted to find that this attractive young woman is her fiancé's ward. Her first superficial offer of friendship (p. 290) quickly turns to jealousy and hostility. She expresses herself bluntly – another resemblance to her mother – but manages to preserve a sophisticated appearance of self-control almost to the end, when Jack enters (p. 294). Gwendolen's sudden alliance with Cecily is as shallow as her first offer of friendship. When Jack and Algernon vow that their lies sprang from love, Gwendolen is openly sceptical – but she intends to crush her doubts. However, she still clings to her preference for the name Ernest.

More than any other character in the play, Gwendolen indulges in the deliberate cultivation of paradox – that is, two apparently contradictory statements or attitudes. This shows in her behaviour as much as in what she actually says. She handles most situations with an intentionally trivial response – as Wilde himself did. The author invested her with some realistic behaviour patterns, such as standing up to her mother, determination to marry the man she loves, jealousy when she thinks there is another woman in his life. But mostly, she appears to cultivate attitudes for their own sake, whether it is a preference for tea without sugar, or refusal to marry a man who is not called Ernest. 'In matters of grave importance, style, not sincerity, is the vital thing' (p. 301), she observes to Cecily. And above all Gwendolen is a young woman of style.

CECILY

Cecily shares some characteristics with Gwendolen, just as they comically share duet speeches in Acts Two and Three. But there are important differences. Cecily is like Algernon in being very sharp-witted and quick to turn a situation to advantage. Where Gwendolen reflects the mannered, posing side of Wilde, the picture of Cecily in her fantasy life and Algernon's reaction to her draw on the more genuinely romantic and tender aspects of Wilde's nature. (These appear in tales such as *The Happy Prince* and in some of his verse.) However, this feature of Cecily's personality is not over-stressed. She is very witty; she fits in well with the general atmosphere of humorous nonsense that gives the play its unique flavour.

We first see her in the romantic setting of a rose-garden, which prepares us for her love scenes with Algernon. She does not look at all like the hearty, healthy schoolgirl described by Jack (p. 271). We soon learn that neither of these impressions is accurate, although it is certainly true that Cecily is not interested in her lessons. She turns all her ingenuity to postponing the hated German lesson with Miss Prism.

The way in which she prolongs their conversation, flatters Miss Prism, and then plays on the governess's weakness for Dr Chasuble (pp. 275–6), all go to prove that Cecily is clever and full of guile. Like Algernon, she prefers to work on other people, rather than assert herself.

When she intervenes in the quarrel between Jack and 'Ernest' (Algernon) (p. 283) she blackmails Jack into shaking hands with the penitent 'Ernest' and then says in a self-satisfied way that her 'little task of reconciliation is over' (p. 283). She leaves the two 'brothers' alone for the shortest possible time before returning to continue her flirtation with Algernon.

In their second meeting we learn that she has been as anxious to meet him as he has been to meet her. When she insists on writing down Algernon's words in her diary we see that it is vanity and an urge towards fantasy that have made Cecily weave this romance around her guardian's wicked younger brother Ernest. Although, like Gwendolen, she feels that 'it had always been a girlish dream . . . to love someone whose name was Ernest' (p. 288), this does not seem so important to her as the total fantasy of Ernest's courtship, presents and letters. Perhaps this is as well, for, as we find out at the end of the play, this wish is not to be fulfilled in Cecily's case.

Cecily's day-dreams take her into a dimension beyond that of the other characters in the play – that is, she exists beyond and apart from her interaction with them. However, this element is so skilfully blended in that there is no sense of discord.

Cecily's intelligence and wit make her quite capable of dealing with the two sophisticated visitors from London. Algernon is subdued into what, for him, we may call speechless adoration; when Gwendolen appears Cecily is polite to her but not swept so quickly into the same kind of instant and effusive warmth. Later on in the battle of wits between the two young women Cecily holds her own convincingly.

Part of the satire in Act Two is that the country – sentimentalized by town-dwellers as a haven of sincerity and simplicity – is shown to be as artful and artificial as the town. Cecily is more quick-witted than Gwendolen: she knows when to lead the conversation (Miss Prism, pp. 274–5, her Uncle Jack, p. 283) and when it is prudent to be silent (Lady Bracknell, p. 305). The silence is not a sign of submissiveness; Cecily is too adroit to clash with Lady Bracknell directly. But when it seems she will not be able to use Lady Bracknell's gracious permission to marry her nephew until she is thirty-five, Cecily rebels. She has all the impatience of youth. She hates waiting five minutes for anybody: '. . . waiting, even to be married, is quite out of the question' (p. 307), she says.

When Algernon appeals to her asking what is to be done about this final obstacle Cecily withdraws into a formal 'I don't know, Mr Moncrieff.' Except for a brief remark to Gwendolen she does not speak again. When the three sets of lovers are united, all except Cecily voice their pleasure at this happy conclusion. Cecily is the only character not to have her wishes granted: she does not get her Ernest. This unresolved point is a weakness in the construction of the play, but Wilde carries us through it by the happy exuberance of the ending.

MISS PRISM

The oldish spinster still eager for love and marriage was a familiar figure in Victorian comic opera and pantomime. The tradition is also found in Sheridan and the Restoration playwrights. In *The Importance of Being Earnest* she is treated more kindly than her predecessors, and mature love is requited.

We laugh at what Miss Prism says because she is quite unaware of the comic effect she is creating. She is not deliberately witty as are Algernon and Cecily. She is fussily conscientious about her duties, repeatedly urging Cecily to study hard (p. 276), but easily distracted by her artful pupil, who plays on her weakness for Dr Chasuble to postpone the hated German lesson (p. 276). She is inclined to make severe moral judgements, expressing strong disapproval of the wicked Ernest, whom she condemns as 'irretrievably weak and vacillating' (p. 275). Unlike Cecily she is not eager to see him reformed. 'As a man sows, so let him reap' (p. 275) she says sternly. When she hears of Ernest's 'death' (p. 280) she does not try to comfort Jack as Dr Chasuble does, but comments, 'What a lesson for him! I trust he will profit by it' (p. 280).

Miss Prism is very prim and proper. Any reference to sex is delicately shrouded in *euphemism* — that is, wrapped up in elaborate phrases. The poor do not 'seem to know what thrift is' (p. 281) — in other words, how to be careful when spending money. She means they have more babies than they can afford, a ridiculous statement in the days before reliable means of birth control were generally available. Dr Chasuble's refusal to marry 'leads weaker vessels astray' (arouses sexual attraction) (p. 279).

The name Prism is itself a sly joke. It was one of the words that Victorian girls were advised to practise often, to give their lips the desired rosebud shape. (Remember Cecily's remark that after her German lesson she looks 'quite plain' (p. 274).)

Wilde also pokes fun at Miss Prism's limited knowledge. She is puzzled by Dr Chasuble's classical and theological allusions and offends his scholarly soul by her barbaric coining of the word 'womanthrope' (p. 279). *Misanthrope* derives from two Greek words, the first meaning 'hate' and the second 'human being' — as in *anthropology*, the study of mankind. Miss Prism assumes that *misan-* is a corruption of 'man' and that *-thrope* means 'hate'. *Neologistic* (another Greek derivation) refers to the coining of new words. We see that despite her devotion to German grammar Miss Prism has little grasp of the roots of language.

Underneath her conventional exterior Miss Prism is as romantic as Cecily. She is strongly attracted to Dr Chasuble and pursues him remorselessly, although she is guarded in the way in which she voices her feelings. Her romantic side is also shown by her early literary ambitions. She had been so absorbed in the world of her three-volume novel that she substituted it for the baby she was supposed to be looking after (p. 310). We can guess at the nature of Miss Prism's dream-world from her pronouncement that in her story 'The good ended happily, and the bad unhappily. That is what Fiction means' (p. 275). With this remark Wilde superbly hits off both the governess's limited mental vision and the tendency of his age to prefer moral uplift to realism in its literature.

Miss Prism has a most important part to play in the plot, since she unwittingly holds the clue to the secret of Jack's birth. In the scene with Lady Bracknell, where this is divulged, more is shown of her character. She is cowed and nervous when her former employer confronts her (p. 309), but she does, however, display indignation when her cherished novel is dismissed as a 'manuscript . . . of more than usually revolting sentimentality' (p. 309), and again when Jack supposes she is his unmarried mother (p. 311).

Miss Prism is slower than the other characters to recognize the significance of what is happening when Jack brings in her hand-bag. When asked to identify it she immediately goes on a memory trip to recall the small, trivial incidents of her youth. She ends complacently, 'I am delighted to have it so unexpectedly restored to me. It has been a great inconvenience being without it all these years' (p. 311).

DR CHASUBLE

Dr Chasuble is the clergyman in charge of the local parish church, the Rector. He is also a Doctor of Divinity (D.D.), and holds office at some nearby cathedral as a canon—hence his various titles in the play. His name is another pun: a chasuble is a sleeveless garment worn by a priest when celebrating Mass or Communion. Dr Chasuble is a caricature of a plummy-voiced, self-satisfied country clergyman, full of unworldly sentiment but living in great comfort.

His eventual union with Miss Prism is prepared for by the way in which their attitudes and values agree. They both disapprove of 'Ernest' and praise the apparent serious-mindedness of his brother Jack. The Canon shows more generosity when he hears of Ernest's 'death' and gently reprimands Miss Prism for her harshness. 'Charity, dear Miss Prism, charity! None of us are perfect' (p. 280).

From the description of his all-purpose sermon we gather that Dr Chasuble's religious feelings are sincere but not deeply troublesome to him. He is quite satisfied with the world as he finds it, apart from the distressing way the poorer classes insist on over-producing themselves (p. 282).

Dr Chasuble is involved with the plot only through the intended christenings – although in fact these never take place. He pulls less weight than the other characters, but he is necessary as a counterpart to Miss Prism. His high-flown language, funny in itself, forms a delightful contrast to the conversation of the four young lovers, and he himself adds most amusingly to Wilde's picture of the deceptively 'simple' country as opposed to the sophisticated town.

THE SERVANTS

Merriman, Jack's butler, is a conventional servant figure. He is there to provide a realistic picture of the pampered idleness against which the main characters play out their whims and deceptions. Merriman's restraining presence heightens the comedy of the scene between Gwendolen and Cecily, in which real emotions struggle against conventional good manners.

Lane, Algernon's manservant, is more of an individual. He echoes his master's detachment and poise. His comments are important in setting the tone of the scene when the play opens. When Algernon accuses him of stealing his champagne Lane is ready with an answer (p. 253) and, moreover, turns aside the possibility of there being any real investigation into his misbehaviour. He loyally comes to Algernon's rescue when Lady Bracknell asks for her promised cucumber sandwiches (p. 261). Lane's unromantic views on marriage give us a foretaste of the equally unromantic and mercenary attitudes that surface among his 'betters' during the course of the play.

Commentary

OSCAR WILDE AND NINETEENTH CENTURY DRAMA

When Wilde's four social comedies were staged in the 1890s, the British theatre was just about to reach the culmination of the process of recovery that resulted in what was known as 'the New Drama'. Over most of the previous hundred years there had been a sharp divergence between literature and plays written for the stage. No major Victorian poet or novelist wrote for the commercial theatre, although many of them – Dickens in particular – were passionately interested in the world of drama.

The two main reasons for this were the debased taste of the audiences and the lack of secure copyright arrangements. Until 1887 there was no really satisfactory means of preventing scripts from being 'pirated'. The result was that during most of its existence Victorian drama took the form of extravagant spectacle, melodrama and adaptations from French plays, or burlesque, which parodies some lofty theme by treating it in a trivial way – as with Offenbach's operetta *Orpheus in the Underworld* (1858) – or makes us laugh at some quite ordinary string of incidents by handling them in inappropriately lofty language. The Savoy opera, *Patience*, is a burlesque. Well-made plays were staged but they had no literary merit and frequently the scripts were not even published. Revivals of Shakespeare were popular although the text was modified to suit public taste.

During the 1860s this situation began to change. The rowdier elements of the audience drifted away to the emerging music halls, where their lively relationship with the performers was more appreciated. There was also a great surge of theatre building: theatres became smaller, better lit (electricity began to be introduced from 1881), and the floor of the auditorium, the pit, was partly taken over by the more exclusive orchestra stalls. To encourage the audience to pay more serious attention the auditorium was darkened during performances, and proper theatre programmes began to take the place of the smudgy, casually produced play-bill. The most important innovation was that the performance was reduced to one major item, instead of the miscellaneous collection of different types of drama that had been usual.

These and other changes were brought in gradually over twenty to thirty years by several talented actor-managers who ran the major London theatres and usually starred in the plays they put on. The best known is Henry Irving, who appeared at the Lyceum with the famous actress Ellen Terry. They alternated performances of Shakespeare with melodrama, for the public still liked strong, moralizing story-lines in its plays.

During this period the social status of actors rose – Irving was knighted in 1895 – and the fashionable world began to flock to the theatre again after a lengthy absence. The curtain now rose much later to fit in with the dinner hour of the upper classes, who were not prepared to sit through the enormously long entertainments of earlier years.

The plays aimed at this more discriminating public began to change in character. The action was set amid upper-class society but the themes and situations struck home to all parts of the audience. They were drawn from the traditional material of melodrama – guilty secrets, compromising letters, double or mistaken identity and women with a shady past. In many of these productions there was a new note of social awareness and questioning that caused the label 'problem play' to be attached to them. Pinero's *The Second Mrs Tanqueray* is one of the earliest and the best known of this emerging kind of drama.

Simultaneously the old types of farce, pantomime, musical extravaganza and comic opera continued to appear, the best known of the last being the Savoy Operas of Gilbert and Sullivan. Smaller, non-commercial theatres were also introducing the great Norwegian dramatist, Henrik Ibsen, in English translations, and there, too, George Bernard Shaw was occasionally finding an outlet for his first dramatic attempts. Both these playwrights had to wait for the new century for their work to become generally acceptable.

It was Pinero and Wilde who first began to reconcile drama and literature, in plays that could be read with pleasure on their own merits and take their place beside the great dramatists of the past. The sparkling wit and satire of Wilde's social dramas make them the first examples of the comedy of manners to achieve literary style and status since Sheridan's *School for Scandal* (1777).

Wilde's characters, situations and plots conform closely to those found in contemporary farce and melodrama. To modern taste there is a strong clash between the brilliant dialogue on one hand and the sensational plot and contrived situations on the other. This applies even to *An Ideal Husband*, where the theme of political corruption has worn rather better than some of the other problems aired.

It is not necessary to read Wilde's other plays to enjoy *The Importance of Being Earnest*, but it would be a good idea to look at one other at least. This would help considerably towards your understanding of the merits that have helped Wilde's last comedy to survive his others. In it, Wilde joyously parodies and 'sends up' the very topics and situations which he handles so seriously in his other plays. The woman with a past, barred from society, is transmuted into the comic Miss Prism; the hypocrisy of fashionable society is mercilessly satirized, but with a lightness of touch that provokes continual laughter, and is far more effective than the priggish outburst of the young American heroine in *A Woman of No Importance*.

The tone of the play owes something to the Savoy Operas. Some of the incidents can even be traced to an early play by Gilbert, *Engaged* (1877), but Wilde's blending of wit, inspired nonsense and sheer good humour are entirely his own, and the harmony between content and structure makes the play a unique achievement in English drama.

BALANCE AND CONTRAST

One of the most striking features of *The Importance of Being Earnest* is the number of parallel or contrasting themes that run through the play. This use of pattern and repetition heightens the artificial atmosphere and adds to our pleasure in the nonsensical dialogue.

We will look at a few examples that come under this heading. You should be able to find others for yourself.

Firstly, all the characters are paired from the beginning, except for Lady Bracknell, who is the figurehead of the play. Within the sextet of lovers, Jack and Gwendolen with Algernon and Cecily, full of youthful wit and energy, are contrasted with the more sedate Miss Prism and Dr Chasuble. Certain attributes overlap among these characters. Both Gwendolen and Cecily long to marry a man named Ernest; both Jack and Algernon have invented an imaginary figure through whom they may escape irksome social duties – Jack going up to town, while Algernon makes his flight to the country. Cecily's diary and Miss Prism's novel indicate that they both turn to a fantasy life in literature.

Certain scenes appear to be duplicated deliberately with variations. There is a tea party in Act One, and another in Act Two. Lady Bracknell interviews Jack in Acts One and Three (the differences have been examined in the detailed summary of Act Three). There are many parallels in the two courtship scenes (Acts One and Two), and many contrasted groupings of the characters (particularly in Act Two), which have already been discussed.

There are several pairs of general themes contrasted throughout the play: romantic love and mercenary marriage, appearance and reality (the changing relationship of Gwendolen and Cecily: the identity of Ernest; Jack's discovery that his lies have been truthful all the time), town and country (a false and deceptive contrast, as we have seen).

Last, in the dialogue there are numerous examples of deliberate repetition or echoing: the remarks of Miss Prism and Dr Chasuble (p. 276 and p. 279); the comments on Mary Farquhar (p. 259 and p. 262) made by Algernon and Lady Bracknell respectively; the exchanges of Gwendolen and Cecily (p. 292); Jack and Algernon's question, 'What could have put such an idea into your pretty little head?' (p. 294 and p. 295). An elaborate example is (p. 302):

GWENDOLEN: Where questions of self-sacrifice are concerned, men are infinitely beyond us.

CECILY: They have moments of physical courage of which
                 we women know absolutely nothing.

Other examples of repetition will be found in the section on 'The Wit
of Oscar Wilde' (p. 79).

HIGH SOCIETY, ETIQUETTE AND SCANDAL

Wilde's social comedies all draw their characters from the wealthy,
upper-class circles in which he moved during his years of fame.
The activities of this exclusive society, as in any age, were of deep
interest to those not lucky enough to be part of it. However, without the benefit of modern media it was not possible for outsiders
to burrow as deeply as they can today into this society's private
life. Moreover, its lifestyle was much more separate from the rest
of the community.

The nearest the general public got to this area of privilege was
either through dramatic representation or as spectators of the ceremonies and goings to and fro during the London Season. This
extended from spring until the end of summer. Then, except for
weekend visits, Society abandoned its country houses and diverted
itself in town. In the late autumn the upper classes would return to
the country for shooting and hunting, and next year the whole process
would begin again.

Apart from amusement, the main point of the Season was for these
wealthy families to 'bring out' their unmarried daughters — probably
including a presentation to the monarch at Court — so that they could
display themselves at various social functions and find suitable
husbands. Society hostesses had a key role to play in this ritual, which
Wilde caricatures in the behaviour of Lady Bracknell.

By the end of the nineteenth century the landed aristocracy had
been forced by agricultural depression to open their ranks to wealthy
merchants and industrialists — the 'purple of commerce' referred to
by Lady Bracknell (p. 267). (Purple is a colour associated with high
social rank, so this speech emphasizes the growing acceptability of the
world of trade to the aristocracy.) Society had an ambiguous attitude

to these invaders, eager to marry their wealth on one hand and on the other affecting to despise their lack of aristocratic background.

Many handbooks were published throughout the period giving advice on the exacting rules of correct social behaviour, or etiquette, for those anxious to forget their origins. Some of these rules were based on fundamental consideration for others, but a great many were mere whims of fashion.

Certain accepted rules between the sexes we should also find extremely odd today. Unmarried girls from upper-class families never worked for their living and were never seen at social events without their mothers or some married woman to 'chaperone' them. First-name terms between young men and women were considered 'fast' – that is, unless they were related, at least as cousins. That is why Gwendolen addresses Algernon – or 'Algy' as even she calls him – in a familiar way, but Jack remains Mr Worthing until they are engaged.

Married women had much more freedom, but even there, friendships which today we would find quite insignificant could lead to scandal and suspicions of sexual attraction. A woman with a 'past' – someone who had actually had a love affair outside her marriage and possibly left her home and children for it – would lose her place in society. No respectable woman would receive her at her home or be seen with her. There was a hypocritical double standard about this – 'one law for men, and another for women' (p. 311) as Jack puts it – for men did not suffer the same social disgrace. Each of Wilde's society comedies contains a 'woman with a past'. In *The Importance of Being Earnest* this is reduced to the absurdity of Miss Prism's having 'abandoned' Jack as a baby through obsession with her three-volume novel.

Sexual irregularity in a man was less frowned on, so long as it occurred discreetly. Usually, cheating at cards or something shady in his financial dealings was considered far worse. It must be said, though, that anything too notorious could break a man's career, which is what happened to the Irish statesman Charles Stewart Parnell, who was ruined by proof of his adultery in a much publicized divorce suit. Wilde was keenly interested in his case and attended the court hearings. However, a potentially scandalous situation could sometimes be tolerated if the persons involved were powerful enough. In such a case Society closed ranks against outsiders, although it was difficult to stop all rumours. The Prince of Wales (the future Edward VII) whiled away his long apprenticeship to the throne with some notorious love affairs. His mistresses were accepted by Society because of his powerful protection.

It is not surprising that envious curiosity led to the situation where scandalous goings-on among the aristocracy formed a main ingredient in many a Victorian melodrama. In the black-and-white morality of the convention, exposure would lead to utter ruin, and the threat of this gave suspense to the plot.

This was the scheme of ideas that Wilde imported into his social dramas and tragically played out in his own life. In his first three comedies the threat of scandal is used quite unoriginally. He follows the dramatic fashion of his day, although, needless to say, all ends happily. In *The Importance of Being Earnest* the secrets are absurd in themselves, and lead to hilarious absurdity in the action. They are neither threatening nor painful.

THE WIT OF OSCAR WILDE

Wilde himself said that this play was written by a butterfly for butterflies, and any attempt to analyse its froth of wit and nonsense may be likened to sending a rhinoceros in pursuit of a butterfly. However, a few tools of criticism can be helpful in trying to write about its merits. In proportion to what he wrote Oscar Wilde is probably the most widely quoted author after Shakespeare. This is because of the myriad of epigrams that sparkled off his pen.

An *epigram* is a striking remark that amuses because it 'says much in little' and often surprises us into a novel point of view on something. Wilde quite deliberately collected his own witty sayings and those of other people so that he could put them into his plays. There is a story that a friend of his once made a particularly clever remark and Wilde said enviously, 'I wish I had said that.' 'You will, Oscar, you will!' was the quick reply.

There are several kinds of epigram. Wilde's are frequently a variation on some well-known phrase, for example, 'It is a very ungentlemanly thing to read a private cigarette case' (p. 256), where 'cigarette case' is substituted for 'letter'; 'Divorces are made in heaven' (p. 255), instead of 'marriages', '. . . in married life three is company and two is none' (p. 260) – a reversal of the usual belief; 'I hear her hair has turned quite gold from grief' (p. 261) instead of 'white'.

A feature of the epigram is *antithesis*, where one word or phrase is very carefully balanced against another. Antithesis can lengthen an epigram to the point where it loses its crispness, but Wilde worked up this type into some of his most famous quotations. 'All women become like their mothers. That is their tragedy. No man does. That's his' (p. 270).

Today we consider *punning* rather childish, and it is found mostly in newspaper headlines. As a form of humour it was very dear to the Victorians. There are some notable examples in the play – beginning and ending of course, with the title. Wilde uses a great many extended puns – for example, the exploding of poor Mr Bunbury, which has already been discussed. 'Abandoned' and 'lost' are two words that he also uses in this way. Simple examples are, 'It is very vulgar to talk like a dentist when one isn't a dentist. It produces a false impression' (p. 258); 'Only relatives, or creditors, ever ring in that Wagnerian fashion' (p. 260). You need to know something of the history of opera to work that one out! The composer Richard Wagner (1813–1883) produced a series of operas on a grand and heroic scale, known collectively as *The Ring of the Nibelung*.

Parody is used from time to time: to parody something is to write an exaggerated imitation of it. When Algernon tells Cecily that he loves her 'wildly, passionately, devotedly, hopelessly', he is parodying the style of the romantic hero. Wilde's parodies, however, are always perfectly controlled. Algernon *has* fallen in love with Cecily and the enthusiastic outburst contributes to Wilde's satire on romantic love without crushing the delicate thread of romance he has also managed to weave into their relationship.

Other examples of parody are the recognition scene where Jack thinks that Miss Prism is his mother, and practically every speech of Dr Chasuble, who is a 'take-off' of the kind of clergyman who cannot be serious without being pompous.

Wilde's desire to amuse and startle leads him naturally into *paradox*. This is an apparently contradictory remark that, on examination, reveals a deeper truth. When Lady Bracknell refuses to bow to Jack's blackmail he says, 'Then a passionate celibacy is all that any of us can look forward to' (p. 308). Passion and celibacy are two opposed states of being, but putting them together exactly conveys the frustration of the lovers at that moment. Cecily says to Miss Prism, 'I don't like novels that end happily. They depress me so much' (p. 275). Here we are given a clue to Cecily's yearning for emotional excitement. When Algernon asks for an explanation of the intriguing words inside Jack's cigarette case, he tells his friend, '. . . pray make it improbable' (p. 258). Algernon wants to be amused – a leading trait in his character.

In this play Wilde's talent for *nonsense humour* reaches its height. Broadly speaking, he uses two kinds. There is that so frequently used by Algernon: 'I have a business appointment that I am anxious to miss!' (p. 278), and his excuse for eating the cucumber sandwiches (p. 255); and the equally mannered nonsense of Gwendolen: 'If you are not too long, I will wait here for you all my life' (p. 310), and 'The simplicity of your character makes you exquisitely incomprehensible to me' (p. 272).

Then there is the other kind of nonsense humour where the characters follow the internal logic of their own thoughts without realizing what a comic effect their responses produce. Miss Prism's speeches are full of this. Of the death of Ernest she says, 'What a lesson for him! I trust he will profit by it' (p. 280). Such ludicrous exchanges are not far from the world of Lewis Carroll.

Irony is a rather loose term with a range of meanings. Strictly, it means saying the opposite of what is intended. It is a veiled understatement of what the speaker actually means. It can show itself by pretending to adopt someone else's point of view, or repeating their words emphatically. When Jack says that Cecily is excessively pretty and only eighteen (p. 271), Algernon asks ironically, 'Have you told Gwendolen yet that you have an excessively pretty ward who is only just eighteen?' He means of course that Jack should beware of Gwendolen's jealousy.

A phrase we use, 'the irony of a situation', refers to circumstances, rather than words. 'Dramatic irony' arises where the audience is aware of something that has not yet come to the knowledge of a character or characters in the play. There are numerous examples in *The Importance of Being Earnest*, the most outstanding being Jack's entry in Act Two (p. 280) dressed in deep mourning for the death of 'Ernest'. His conversation with Miss Prism and the Canon is wildly funny, both because he knows that they do not realize how he is tricking them, and because we know that Algernon is indoors with Cecily, pretending to be Ernest, and there is going to be a confrontation very soon.

Sarcasm can be ironic but is usually stronger. It is a bitter taunt or gibe. As it is a crude form of humour it is not often used by Wilde. There is one character by whom it is used very effectively. Lady Bracknell is so outraged by the details of Jack's background that for the moment she is almost unable to speak. She returns to the point several times in her speeches on pages 268–9, and later (p. 303) asks sarcastically, 'Mr Worthing, is Miss Cardew at all connected with any of the larger railway stations in London?'

Satire does not come under the heading of verbal wit, but it may be most conveniently mentioned here. Examples have been picked out in the detailed account of the plot. Satire ridicules people or institutions that the author wishes us to laugh at and despise. It is one of the unifying elements of this play and occurs in every episode. Wilde's satire is of a good-humoured kind, and very general. The mechanics of the plot and much of the dialogue poke fun at the dramatic conventions of the day, and also at its literature, education, culture, current notions of propriety and impropriety, relations between servants and employers, sentimental notions about the simplicity of the country and romantic love. The two main targets are social hypocrisy and the mercenary marriage-market of high society.

One form of humour that is notably absent from the *The Importance of Being Earnest* is the broad sexual remark that features so largely in Restoration comedies. The spirit of the age did not find sexual innuendo acceptable – at least not for general consumption. Even the innocently earthy comments of Shakespeare's characters such as the Nurse in *Romeo and Juliet* were censored. The nearest to a sexual joke that we find in this play appears in the cross-referenced remarks of Dr Chasuble and Miss Prism ('I would hang upon her lips' (p. 276) and 'Young women are green' (p. 279)). Here each mistakes the other's meaning and the prim and proper respectability of these middle-aged lovers heightens the absurdity of the mistake.

Glossary

Abstraction: absent-mindedness

Albany: expensive flats near Piccadilly

Alluring: attractive

Anabaptists: a Christian sect believing in adult baptism

Analogy: similarity or correspondence

Apprised: informed

Army Lists: directories containing alphabetical lists of officers in various regiments, published annually

Authenticity: genuineness

Bangle: bracelet

Bankruptcy Court: legal court dealing with cases relating to debt

Bassinette: the same as *perambulator*

Bayswater: a western district of London

Belgrave Square: a fashionable London square

Book: book used for household accounts and bills, here the 'wine book'

Butler: the head servant in a household

Buttonhole: i.e. a flower to put in the lapel of a coat

Canon: a clergyman who is connected with a cathedral

Canonical: in accordance with the regulations of the Church

Card: visiting card printed with one's name, and presented when going to someone's house

Celibacy, celibate: used here in the sense of remaining unmarried

Condolence: sympathy expressed for the grief of others

Constitution: general state of one's health

Court Guides: lists of those presented to the Queen at Court

Credulity: trust, belief

Days of humiliation: days of special church services for proclaiming repentance

D.D.: Doctor of Divinity (with a degree in theology)

Demeanour: appearance, manner

Dog-cart: a light, one-horse wagon

Domesticity: an informal shortening or changing of a name – for example, Algy for Algernon, Jimmy for James

Dressing-case: a case for toilet articles, such as hairbrushes, etc.

Eccentric: odd in behaviour

Effeminate: behaving like a woman

Effrontery: impertinence, impudence, 'cheek'

Egeria: a nymph who according to legend instructed the ancient Roman king, Numa

Empire: a London music hall

Equanimity: calmness of mind

Evensong: evening service at a church

Exotic: rare and strange

Exploded: rejected or found out

Forte: a strong point or something one is good at; also the instruction for a loud tone in music

Forward: impertinent, 'cheeky'

Funds: Government securities, considered a safe investment for money.

German scepticism: a school of philosophy which doubted the possibility of real knowledge

Gorgon: Three monstrous sisters in Greek mythology. The best-known, Medusa, turned people to stone if they looked at her

Grosvenor Square: a fashionable part of London

Hand-bag: a piece of luggage like a sports-bag

Heretical: not in accordance with the agreed doctrines of the church

Horticulturally: connected with the growing of flowers, fruits and vegetables

J.P.: Justice of the Peace, a local magistrate

Immersion: dipping of the whole body in water

Indecorous: undignified

Insuperable: not to be overcome, unconquerable

Irrevocable: not to be changed, unchangeable

Lax: not strict enough in one's moral code

Leamington: a spa town in the Midlands of England

Legislation: the passing of laws

Liberal Unionist: a group of Liberal Members of Parliament who joined the Conservatives in 1886 because they disagreed with Gladstone's policy of Home Rule for Ireland

Lorgnette: spectacles held by a single handle rather than worn

Machinations: plots, intrigues

Manna: referring to an incident in the Old Testament, where the Israelites were miraculously fed in the Wilderness (Exodus 16)

Maréchal Niel: a type of yellow rose

Metaphor: a figure of speech that implies rather than states a comparison between two things

Metaphysical: abstract, philosophical

Metropolitan: connected with London

Misanthrope: one who dislikes fellow human beings in general

Momentary: temporary, not lasting long

Morbid, morbidity: unwholesome in mental outlook

Morning-room: the room where most social activity took place up until the evening dinner

Mudie: a circulating library that sent out books to subscribers

Muffin: a light, spongy cake eaten toasted and buttered

Off colour: unwell

Ordeal: test, challenge

Ostentatiously: in an obvious or showy manner

Oxonian: someone who has attended the University of Oxford

Pagan: here means Greek or Roman

Perambulator: a baby's 'pram'

Perrier-Jouet '89: name of a fine wine, bottled in 1889

Pew-opener: an attendant who showed people to their pews (bench seats) in a church

Philanthropic: connected with charity work – at this time in particular among the people of London's East End

Philistine: one who despises art and culture

Portmanteau: a travelling bag for carrying clothing, etc.

Premature: too early or hasty

Primitive Church: the Christian Church during its earliest years

Prior: earlier

Profligate: dissipated, debauched, vicious or immoral

Quail: tremble, shake

Quixotic: resembling Cervantes' hero, Don Quixote, absurdly generous or unselfish

Radical: very 'left wing' in politics

Ready money: money available to pay bills at once, as distinct from 'credit'

Reception: a society evening entertainment

Reconciliation: reuniting of people who have quarrelled

Rector: a clergyman in charge of a parish church

Relapse: return of an illness

Rupee: unit of Indian currency

Salver: tray

Scotland Yard: police headquarters in London

Secular: irreverent, irreligious

Semi-recumbent: half lying down

Sent down: i.e. to the dining room from the drawing room, where guests were received before dinner

Shilly-shallying: hesitation, indecision

Smoking jacket: a special coat worn by men when smoking, to avoid the smell of tobacco clinging to the evening coat

Superciliously: in a sneering manner

Susceptible: affected by

Tableau: a striking or dramatic situation, a taking-up of attitudes on the stage so as to form a picture without movement

Tea-cake: a light kind of cake

Temperance beverage: non-alcoholic drink, e.g. lemonade

Thrift: economy, carefulness over the spending of money

Trivet: three-legged stand for pot or kettle; *right as a trivet* – perfectly dependable

Tutelage: the stage of being under age, needing a guardian

Utilitarian: practical or useful

University Extension Scheme: system of university lectures intended for the general public

Vacillating: indecisive, hesitating

Vestry: part of a church in which the records, vessels and robes worn by the clergy are kept

Vicinity: neighbourhood, locality

Willis's: a fashionable restaurant of the day

Examination Questions

If you are studying for the G.C.S.E. examination you may find that the set texts have been selected by your teacher from a very wide list of suggestions in the examination syllabus. The questions in the examination paper will therefore be applicable to many different books. Here are some possible questions that you could answer by making use of *The Importance of Being Earnest*.

1. Give an account of a play you have read or seen performed in which wit is an important element. What does it achieve?

2. The opening scene of a play is extremely important. Describe the opening of a play in which many of the characters and themes are introduced to the audience, and indicate how these are developed as the action proceeds. You may like to compare the later action to the opening.

3. Discuss a play in which the confusion of identities is an important element. What does such confusion provide over and above pure comedy?

4. Differences of social class are important to many plays. Discuss a play in which such differences make a major contribution to the action.

5. Many works of literature have marriage as a central theme. Choose a play in which this is so and show the relation of marriage to love, money and social ambition.

6.   Plays written in societies other than our own require some knowledge of the lives of the people for whom they were first written. Choose a play first performed over fifty years ago and show knowledge of how ways of life different from our own are important to understanding it.

7.   Many comic characters are really caricatures. Describe two or more characters from a play who seem to you to fit this description.

8.   Many plays are dependent on the unravelling of a mystery for their effect. Discuss a play in which this is important.

FOR THE BEST IN PAPERBACKS, LOOK FOR THE 🐧

PENGUIN DICTIONARIES

Archaeology
Architecture
Art and Artists
Biology
Botany
Building
Chemistry
Civil Engineering
Commerce
Computers
Decorative Arts
Design and Designers
Economics
English and European
  History
English Idioms
Geography
Geology
Historical Slang
Literary Terms
Mathematics

Microprocessors
Modern History 1789–1945
Modern Quotations
Physical Geography
Physics
Political Quotations
Politics
Proverbs
Psychology
Quotations
Religions
Saints
Science
Sociology
Surnames
Telecommunications
The Theatre
Troublesome Words
Twentieth Century History

Dictionaries of all these – and more – in Penguin

The Age of Reason   Jean-Paul Sartre

The first part of Sartre's classic trilogy, set in the volatile Paris summer of 1938, is itself 'a dynamic, deeply disturbing novel' (Elizabeth Bowen) which tackles some of the major issues of our time.

Three Lives   Gertrude Stein

A turning point in American literature, these portraits of three women – thin, worn Anna, patient, gentle Lena and the complicated, intelligent Melanctha – represented in 1909 one of the pioneering examples of modernist writing.

Doctor Faustus   Thomas Mann

Perhaps the most convincing description of an artistic genius ever written, this portrait of the composer Leverkuhn is a classic statement of one of Mann's obsessive themes: the discord between genius and sanity.

The New Machiavelli   H. G. Wells

This autobiography of a man who has thrown up a glittering political career and marriage to go into exile with the woman he loves also contains an illuminating Introduction by Melvyn Bragg.

The Collected Poems of Stevie Smith

Amused, amusing and deliciously barbed, this volume includes many poems which dwell on death; as a whole, though, as this first complete edition in paperback makes clear, Smith's poetry affirms an irrepressible love of life.

Rhinoceros / The Chairs / The Lesson   Eugène Ionesco

Three great plays by the man who was one of the founders of what has come to be known as the Theatre of the Absurd.

The Second Sex Simone de Beauvoir

This great study of Woman is a landmark in feminist history, drawing together insights from biology, history and sociology as well as literature, psychoanalysis and mythology to produce one of the supreme classics of the twentieth century.

The Bridge of San Luis Rey Thornton Wilder

On 20 July 1714 the finest bridge in all Peru collapsed, killing 5 people. Why? Did it reveal a latent pattern in human life? In this beautiful, vivid and compassionate investigation, Wilder asks some searching questions in telling the story of the survivors.

Parents and Children Ivy Compton-Burnett

This richly entertaining introduction to the world of a unique novelist brings to light the deadly claustrophobia within a late-Victorian upper-middle-class family . . .

Vienna 1900 Arthur Schnitzler

These deceptively languid sketches, four 'games with love and death', lay bare an astonishing and disturbing world of sexual turmoil (which anticipates Freud's discoveries) beneath the smooth surface of manners and convention.

Confessions of Zeno Italo Svevo

Zeno, an innocent in a corrupt world, triumphs in the end through his stoic acceptance of his own failings in this extraordinary, experimental novel which fuses memory, obsession and desire.

The House of Mirth Edith Wharton

Lily Bart – beautiful, intelligent and charming – is trapped like a butterfly in the inverted jam jar of wealthy New York society . . . This tragic comedy of manners was one of Wharton's most shocking and innovative books.

FOR THE BEST IN PAPERBACKS, LOOK FOR THE

PENGUIN REFERENCE BOOKS

The Penguin English Dictionary

Over 1,000 pages long and with over 68,000 definitions, this cheap, compact and totally up-to-date book is ideal for today's needs. It includes many technical and colloquial terms, guides to pronunciation and common abbreviations.

The Penguin Reference Dictionary

The ideal comprehensive guide to written and spoken English the world over, with detailed etymologies and a wide selection of colloquial and idiomatic usage. There are over 100,000 entries and thousands of examples of how words are actually used – all clear, precise and up-to-date.

The Penguin English Thesaurus

This unique volume will increase anyone's command of the English language and build up your word power. Fully cross-referenced, it includes synonyms of every kind (formal or colloquial, idiomatic and figurative) for almost 900 headings. It is a must for writers and utterly fascinating for any English speaker.

The Penguin Dictionary of Quotations

A treasure-trove of over 12,000 new gems and old favourites, from Aesop and Matthew Arnold to Xenophon and Zola.

The Penguin Guide to the Law

This acclaimed reference book is designed for everyday use, and forms the most comprehensive handbook ever published on the law as it affects the individual.

The Penguin Medical Encyclopedia

Covers the body and mind in sickness and in health, including drugs, surgery, history, institutions, medical vocabulary and many other aspects. 'Highly commendable' – *Journal of the Institute of Health Education*

The Penguin French Dictionary

This invaluable French-English, English-French dictionary includes both the literary and dated vocabulary needed by students, and the up-to-date slang and specialized vocabulary (scientific, legal, sporting, etc) needed in everyday life. As a passport to the French language, it is second to none.

A Dictionary of Literary Terms

Defines over 2,000 literary terms (including lesser known, foreign language and technical terms) explained with illustrations from literature past and present.

The Penguin Map of Europe

Covers all land eastwards to the Urals, southwards to North Africa and up to Syria, Iraq and Iran. Scale – 1:5,500,000, 4-colour artwork. Features main roads, railways, oil and gas pipelines, plus extra information including national flags, currencies and populations.

The Penguin Dictionary of Troublesome Words

A witty, straightforward guide to the pitfalls and hotly disputed issues in standard written English, illustrated with examples and including a glossary of grammatical terms and an appendix on punctuation.

FOR THE BEST IN PAPERBACKS, LOOK FOR THE

PENGUIN PASSNOTES

This comprehensive series, designed to help O-level and CSE students, includes:

SUBJECTS
Biology
Chemistry
Economics
English Language
French
Geography
Human Biology
Mathematics
Modern Mathematics
Modern World History
Narrative Poems
Physics

SHAKESPEARE
As You Like It
Henry IV, Part I
Henry V
Julius Caesar
Macbeth
The Merchant of Venice
A Midsummer Night's Dream
Romeo and Juliet
Twelfth Night

LITERATURE
Arms and the Man
Cider With Rosie
Great Expectations
Jane Eyre
Kes
Lord of the Flies
A Man for All Seasons
The Mayor of Casterbridge
My Family and Other Animals
Pride and Prejudice
The Prologue to The Canterbury
  Tales
Pygmalion
Saint Joan
She Stoops to Conquer
Silas Marner
To Kill a Mockingbird
War of the Worlds
The Woman in White
Wuthering Heights